Endangered Recipes

Endangered Recipes

Too Good to Be Forgotten

LARI ROBLING

PHOTOGRAPHS BY **MARK THOMAS**

STEWART, TABORI & CHANG
NEW YORK

The recipe for Chopped Chicken Livers on page 17 is from *The Molly Goldberg Jewish Cookbook* by Gertrude Berg and
Myra Waldo. It is reprinted with the permission of Ivyland Books, 7 Solebury Mountain Road, New Hope, PA 18938
ISBN: 0-9669833-0-0

Page 2: Sticky Buns (recipe on page 90)

Published in 2003 by
Stewart, Tabori & Chang
A Company of La Martinière Groupe
115 West 18th Street
New York, NY 10011

Export Sales to all countries except Canada, France,
and French-speaking Switzerland:
Thames and Hudson Ltd.
181A High Holborn
London WC1V 7QX
England

Canadian Distribution:
Canadian Manda Group
One Atlantic Avenue, Suite 105
Toronto, Ontario M6K 3E7
Canada

Library of Congress Cataloging-in-Publication Data
Robling, Lari.
    Endangered recipes : too good to be forgotten / Lari Robling ; photographs by Mark Thomas.
        p.   cm.
    ISBN: 1-58479-312-0
    1. Cookery, American. I. Title.
    TX715.R6543 2003
    641.5973—dc21   2003050464

Designed by Laura Lindgren

The text of this book was composed in Cooper Oldstyle, Twentieth Century, and Gaberdine.

Printed in China

10 9 8 7 6 5 4 3 2 1
First Printing

In memory of my grandmothers:
Marie Dugan, who taught me how to cook and that there's always "enough";
Maude VanNostran, who told me "with that many expensive
ingredients you can make a whisk broom taste good."

And to my "kids":
Leigh, Ben, Dan, Taylor, and all who follow—
eat frequently and with gusto at the family table!

———— •• ————

Contents

Introduction

*P*erhaps nothing connects us to our past more profoundly than sense memory. And the nostalgic memories stimulated by food are, without a doubt, the most evocative and compelling of all. Tastes, smells, or textures can trigger long-forgotten but significant moments in life, and return us to specific places in time; they are our subliminal train tickets to long-ago destinations. The aroma of a particular dish can take you back to your childhood instantaneously. Suddenly you are racing your bicycle down the block to get home in time for dinner as the smells of familiar ingredients waft from neighborhood kitchens. Or a bite of homemade lumpy mashed potatoes transports you back to comforting Sunday suppers with the whole family gathered around the table. Perhaps your Proustian epiphany is the meal that carries you and your loved one back to the first time you ever cooked together. Now you serve it, rich with meaning, at every anniversary.

Yet, for all we enjoy the connection between what we eat and where we've come from, we are in danger of losing the very recipes that spark those memories. I certainly regret the dishes that got away: my grandmother's baked beans that no one bothered to learn how to make; the dumplings I didn't like as a kid, which now I think I would enjoy. It happens to almost every family. You sit down to a holiday meal and realize that Grandma is the only one who knows the secrets of her biscuits or that special gravy. If you are lucky, you'll re-create the recipes. But with each passing day, as the last generation to truly cook from scratch grows older, we lose many recipes and cooking techniques. Equally sad, we spend less time together with friends and family enjoying the pleasures of the table. And so, this loss of kitchen time and family time reflects an endangered way of life. *Endangered Recipes* is a call to return to the kitchen and spend time cooking together, eating together, and sharing stories.

I began writing this book by wondering, where have all the American classic recipes gone? Dishes such as Welsh rarebit, crab cakes, Green Goddess dressing, and Parker House rolls fell by the wayside in the food revolution of the seventies and eighties. They were replaced with nouvelle cuisine and more global foods, or they became poor imitations of themselves in frozen entrees and bad banquet dinners. It became my goal, indeed my obsession, to bring them back in all their glory. I wondered, too, why so many regional specialties were quickly disappearing. For while Nashville House fried biscuits, barbecue ham, or Pensacola gaspachee salad still have a few loyal fans, surely they deserve a larger audience. Or consider blackened fish; once a regional treasure, it became a pale imitation of itself—a cliché on nearly every restaurant chain menu. The same fate threatens southwestern fare such as chiles rellenos, which is losing its identity in bland or homogenized versions. And what about our ingredients? Today's trend toward healthier eating has nearly banished key items such as lard from our diets—and then we wonder why we can't make biscuits or pie crusts as good as Grandmom's. All these foods must be saved.

But to rescue our culinary past, we need to think about how we've evolved into a culture with too little patience and too few teachers. Many of the recipes I've included, such as delicious treats like apple butter or doughnuts, provide simple reminders of the need to slow down and pay attention when preparing our food. Certainly, we don't have the luxury of cooking this way every day, but we can find the time to spend an afternoon learning to make a special dish. Once a month or so, we can plan a family dinner and spend time preparing and sharing a meal together. Within the guidelines of moderation we can enjoy richer fare, especially when it is eaten slowly and garnished with conversation.

There is, of course, the issue of recording technique. Over time, experienced home cooks have developed particular methods of handling ingredients. Knowing how to test a piece of meat to see if it is done, or using a certain kind of pan to create the best heat are skills that are best learned by observation. Often these techniques have a tradition of being passed down from generation to generation and are part of a family ritual. In this book, I have done my best to translate the specific ways in which certain dishes are prepared.

While I sought out these recipes, I was constantly reminded that cooking is wonderfully idiosyncratic. Standard fare such as macaroni and cheese, brisket, Boston baked beans or noodle kugel vary according to their origin. The mac' and cheese my grandmother made is the taste that will always resonate with me. Your grandmother may have used a white sauce, or a different blend of cheeses to hit the flavor note that strikes your emotional chord. Recording *your* version adds to our culinary orchestra.

In the process of helping others set recipe to paper for this book, I became aware of the many influences on our food. America consists of a diverse population and everyone who has settled here has enriched our culture by bringing their own culinary heritage with them. Assimilation into our culture, however, can mean succeeding generations lose the touch required to turn out the perfect blini or expertly season the kebbeh. A recipe that truly explains the fall activity of brining kimchee, for example, provides an everlasting and vital record of the strong intergenerational bonds that were forged by those who left their homelands to settle in the United States.

While researching this book, I met so many people from all walks of life who had a hunger to learn how to make their childhood dishes: from a favorite Korean steak on fire (bulgogi) to a perfect peach pie. Whether they are home cooks, food writers or restaurateurs, each returns home, time and again, to savor the tastes of their beloved foods. And they are recording and preserving recipes for the next generation. I consider these people true recipe rescuers, the protagonists profiled in the chapters of this book. Like them, you can rescue *your* family recipes from extinction and immortalize the stories they tell.

A Note on the Recipes

While my mission is to record recipes accurately, I have updated many of them to include the use of modern appliances, such as a food processor. I still have, and occasionally use, my grandmother's hand grinder that fastens to the countertop, but she would have been thrilled at the convenience of a food processor. No more grated knuckles when making coleslaw or potato pancakes on a box grater!

Our tastes, as well as our cooking devices, have changed over the decades. In most cases I use olive oil rather than corn oil or butter because of the health benefits attributed to it today. I also use nonstick cooking spray, a modern cooking product that seems to have become indispensable. If a change would affect the dish, such as substituting for lard in a pie crust, I have noted that in the recipe. Similarly, I used 2% milk in most recipes because the change is imperceptible. In those cases where the taste profile is affected the recipes will list whole milk. When I do use butter, I prefer unsalted sweet butter because its flavor is purer. Eggs are assumed to be large eggs which, unlike previous generations, are available year-round.

SUNDAY SUPPERS

*W*hen my uncle and grandfather would go fishing on Saturdays and bring back a real catch, we could count on a Sunday fish fry. The menu for these special Sunday suppers included my grandmother's baked beans and dinner rolls. Six cousins, two sets of parents, and Grandma and Grandpa filled the tiny duplex on Grand Avenue in Akron, Ohio. Several pans of hot oil kept churning out fish fillets in rapid fire order. We ate like there was no tomorrow, and then some.

This Sunday supper tradition led to a major confusion on my part that lasted well until adulthood. The parents worried about the kids choking on fish bones and made a big point of keeping bread and milk within easy reach. Apparently, the cure for choking on a fish bone was to eat a piece of bread and wash it down with milk. I extrapolated from this precaution that eating fish was a dangerous activity and to be done only with extreme prudence. Somehow, I overlooked the fact that the folklore which recommended eating bread and drinking milk while choking lacked a certain understanding of the physiology of breathing and swallowing. I'm happy to report that I now freely eat many different kinds of fish without any regard to first aid or Dr. Heimlich.

Sunday suppers, however, have met their own "bone in the throat." As families spread out across the country and become rootless, the extended family is difficult to gather on a regular basis. Even the nuclear family can't count on eating a traditional Sunday meal together on a regular basis anymore.

What's the difference between a Sunday supper and a dinner? There's a certain amount of local custom and regionalism in the answer. In some religious quarters, the food is sandwiched in between the morning and evening church services. This is what my husband recalls. Rather than having lunch, the heartier dinner meal came after the first service and the lighter supper was often leftovers eaten before going to evening prayer.

Other more rural communities might have a heartier meal early in the day and leave time to take care of evening chores. For my maternal grandfather, there was no such thing as "lunch." Dinner was what you ate after the noon hour, while supper was the last meal of the day, whether it was Sunday or any other day of the week.

A friend recalls his Sunday suppers served in a bowl on a tray in front of a round, seven-inch screen: the television. Ultimately this new media was an advance that abetted the demise of the traditional Sunday suppers, but initially families gathered together around the modern device and invited Jack Benny, Ed Sullivan, and Molly Goldberg into their living rooms. Swanson TV Dinners quickly followed—a small step for food science and mankind's giant leap into the culinary abyss. Still, at least everyone was in the same room and those old variety shows had a jump up on current reality shows as family entertainment.

Sunday supper fare offers a wide range of options. For some, ease of preparation is the hallmark. It could be a simple bowl of stew, a one-dish casserole, or a sandwich. This leaves time to share a movie together or play a board game.

Others opt for more of a production with roast chicken, mashed potatoes, and at least three generations at the table. Admittedly, this takes more time and effort. If the mere thought of this throws you into a mild panic attack, make it a covered-dish affair (also known as potluck or pitch in, depending on what part of the country you live in). You'll be responsible for setting the table and the main hot dish. Everyone else contributes the sides, desserts, and clean-up help.

We don't live near family, so I enjoy inviting a few neighbors over for an afternoon of conversation. When I'm up to it, I like doing a big dinner and spending hours at the table. During the times when writing deadlines have me frenzied, I take a simpler approach. I'll purchase some interesting cheeses paired with a nice wine for a starter, and then I'll thaw out a homemade soup or batch of posole from the freezer. Our conversation and relaxation can comfortably stretch into the evening. The one dish I absolutely must have with a Sunday supper, though, is a homemade pie. Nothing goes down smoother than a cup of coffee and a piece of pie. It is restorative and prepares me for the week ahead.

Whether you have several generations at the table or opt for a quieter meal, these recipes are a Sunday best.

Dublin Colcannon

*M*y grandfather often spoke about a special dish his aunt from Dublin, Ireland, made. He rhapsodized about this dish—cabbage mixed with other ingredients to give it a little sweetness—in the most loving and longing way. Three generations of women tried to re-create the dish of his memory but without success. He said it called for "dark" cabbage, which we thought might be purple cabbage. Try as we might, we made some wonderful cabbage dishes but nothing like his Aunt Sadie's.

Many years later, the mystery was solved when I interviewed Irish cooking authority Darina Allen. Her book, *The Complete Book of Irish Country Cooking*, includes a recipe for Dublin colcannon. As it turns out, the Irish often refer to kale as cabbage. The dish was just as my grandfather described, a lovely mix of dark, tangy greens combined with the sweetness of the parsnips and soft texture of the mashed potatoes. I was lucky to have found it.

I like using russet potatoes. Although Darina peels her potatoes before cooking, my grandmother never peeled them before cooking so I don't either. It's much easier and adds some flavor. Don't skimp on the butter!

1 pound parsnips, washed and peeled

1 pound potatoes, washed but do not peel

1 pound curly kale

1 cup whole milk

2 scallions, coarsely chopped

4 tablespoons butter, plus more for serving

salt and black pepper to taste

Add parsnips and potatoes to a large saucepan and cover with water. Add a pinch of salt and bring to a boil.

Meanwhile, remove the center ribs from the kale leaves and cook in a separate pot of boiling, salted water. Drain well and finely chop. Set aside.

In a small saucepan, bring milk to a simmer and add scallions. Set aside and let steep.

Cook parsnips and potatoes until tender and a fork pierces the center easily. Drain off all the water. Working quickly, peel potatoes. Cut parsnips into 1-inch pieces and add potatoes and parsnips to a large bowl for mashing.

Strain milk, discarding scallions. Add about two-thirds of the milk to parsnips and potatoes and mash with a potato masher. Add butter and more of the milk if necessary. Mix in kale, season with salt and pepper, and serve immediately. An additional lump of butter on top is a nice addition.

SERVES 4

Chopped Chicken Livers

*J*oel Fram became an unwitting recipe rescuer when a relative of his went looking for an out-of-print cookbook she remembered from her childhood. When Fram unearthed a dog-eared copy of *The Molly Goldberg Jewish Cookbook,* he figured lots of women (and men) would remember this gem based on the famous TV character. He bought the rights to reissue the book. Molly Goldberg was the nation's Jewish matriarch for decades. Known for her malaprops and fractured English, Molly's directions include phrases such as "throw an eye on every however" for stir occasionally. Of her chicken livers she says, "try this and I'm sure you'll be an attic like me." Serve this on a bed of lettuce leaves as an appetizer. It is customary to serve it with a tablespoon of rendered chicken fat (schmaltz) over the top.

½ cup shortening or butter	2 hard-cooked egg yolks
2 onions, sliced	1½ teaspoons salt
1 pound chicken livers, washed and drained	¼ teaspoons freshly ground black pepper

Heat ¼ cup of the shortening in a skillet. Add onions and sauté, stirring occasionally, until just starting to turn color. Remove onions and set aside.

Heat remaining shortening in the skillet. Add livers and sauté until no longer red but still tender.

Grind onions, livers, egg yolks, salt, and pepper in a food chopper (Molly cooked before food processors, which work ideally). Refrigerate to chill thoroughly.

MAKES ABOUT 1½ CUPS

Mrs. Small's Crab Cakes

Dorothy Small only gave up this recipe on her death bed, although just about anyone who had been a guest in the Oxford, Maryland, home of Douglas and Lucille Wallop had requested it. Mrs. Small was Lucille's friend and housekeeper and kept the steady flow of New York theater colleagues who visited the couple well fed. I was given this recipe by Lucille's daughter and my friend, biographer Dorothy Herrmann, who recalls that there were many good crab cakes along the Eastern Shore, but none could touch Mrs. Small's.

¼ cup minced onion

4 tablespoons butter, melted

3 tablespoons finely minced parsley

1 egg, unbeaten

2 tablespoons mayonnaise

1 tablespoon Dijon mustard

½ teaspoon salt

¼ teaspoon dry mustard

3 slices white bread, torn into ¼-inch pieces (about 1 cup)

1 pound backfin or jumbo lump crabmeat, picked over for any bits of cartilage

oil, for frying

flour, for dredging

In a medium bowl, blend together onion, butter, parsley, egg, mayonnaise, Dijon mustard, salt, and dry mustard. Add bread and mix well. Gently toss crabmeat into the mix. Form into patties, using about ⅓ cup, tightly packed, per patty. Refrigerate, covered, overnight.

Just before serving, pour enough oil in a heavy frying pan to come 1 inch up the sides. Heat to 375° F, or until it sizzles when a little flour is sprinkled into the pan. Dredge the crab cakes in a little flour and fry for about 2 minutes on the first side and 1 to 2 minutes on the second side, or until browned and heated through.

MAKES ABOUT 8 CAKES, OR 4 MAIN-DISH SERVINGS

Sunday Roast Chicken

To me, the execution of a perfectly hard-cooked egg or a tender-crisp roast chicken is the proof of a good cook. I've always had good success with this formula for roasting a chicken. It works well with a larger bird or oven-stuffer, but you will need to increase the cooking time. I like to add some fresh herbs such as tarragon, marjoram, or thyme, but I encourage you to discover your own favorites. Some people get fancy and stick slices of garlic under the skin before roasting, which may just be a little too much work for a relaxed Sunday afternoon.

1 3½- to 4½-pound whole chicken, rinsed and patted dry

½ lemon or lime

1 tablespoon kosher salt

fresh herbs, if desired

Preheat oven to 400° F.

Place chicken in a shallow roasting pan and squeeze lemon juice on top. Sprinkle salt over chicken. Stuff cavity with juiced lemon rind and, if desired, herbs.

Bake chicken for 1 hour, then check juices to see if they run clear. If not, continue baking an additional 15 minutes and check again.

SERVES 4

Posole

I first tasted this southwestern dish in the cantina of the New Mexican home of my friends Guylyn and Lynn Nusom. It was a chilly fall day and we had just returned from Hatch, New Mexico—known as the chile capital of the world. There we had watched our Big Jim chiles turn in the roaster, just enough to blister the skin. Everywhere we looked the tin roofs of the houses were brightly covered with ripe, red chiles as they dried in the sun. The air was perfumed with the pleasantly smoky and intoxicating aroma of roasted chiles, and the trip home was filled with expectation. We sat in the cantina warming ourselves with hot, steamy bowls of posole accompanied by large dollops of red chile sauce, chunks of avocado, and chopped cilantro. The liquid melody of rain on the tin roof played like Bobby Short at the Carlyle.

Lynn laments that more and more he is seeing this regional specialty dish in a canned version on the supermarket shelves. This is a shame because it is really easy to make and is a hallmark of New Mexican cuisine.

2 tablespoons oil	½ cup fresh roasted green chile or
½ pound lean pork, cut into 1-inch cubes	1 4.5-ounce can
1 medium onion, diced	1 tablespoon crushed red pepper, or
2 cloves garlic, minced	to taste
2 20-ounce cans hominy (about 6 cups)	1 teaspoon dried Mexican oregano
2 cups chicken broth	(see Kitchen Wisdom on page 23)
about 2 cups hot water	½ teaspoon ground cumin

Heat oil in a large skillet or Dutch oven. Sauté pork over medium-high heat until browned, about 3 to 5 minutes. Add onion and garlic. Cook 1 to 2 minutes more until the onion is translucent.

Add hominy, broth, 2 cups water, chile, crushed red pepper, oregano, and cumin. Add more water if necessary to cover the pork and hominy. Simmer over low heat until the pork is tender, 45 minutes to 1 hour.

MAKES ABOUT 8 CUPS

Kitchen Wisdom

If you have a good spice store or Mexican market in your neighborhood, look for Mexican oregano. It has a sweeter, softer flavor than the more common Italian variety. If you can't find Mexican oregano, substitute dried marjoram instead.

———— •• ————

To substitute dried hominy in this recipe, cover one pound of dried hominy with water in a large pot and bring to a boil. Simmer for about two hours until the hominy is soft and cooked through with no hardness in the center. Drain and use in place of the canned hominy. Although it is more difficult to find, cooked hominy also comes refrigerated and ready for use.

Red Chile Sauce

Red chile sauce is the ketchup of the Southwest. It is the classic touch in enchiladas, huevos rancheros, tamales and, of course, posole. And, like most traditions, there is plenty of discussion and disagreement about which is the best and most authentic recipe. I like Guylyn and Lynn Nusom's version with just a touch of tomato paste to balance the flavors. However, native New Mexicans will debate the formula for the best recipe with about as much heat as a hot pepper itself.

15 to 20 dried mild red chiles (about 5 ounces), stemmed	2 tablespoons flour
4 to 5 cups water	1 teaspoon cumin
2 tablespoons oil	1 teaspoon salt
	1 tablespoon tomato paste (optional)

Place chiles in a medium saucepan and add just enough water to cover. Bring to a boil. Reduce heat and simmer uncovered, about 10 minutes. Let cool.

In a blender or food processor, working in small batches, purée chiles with their liquid. Strain through a sieve, discarding any solids.

Heat oil in a heavy saucepan. Add flour and cook for 1 to 2 minutes to make a roux. Add cumin and salt. Add strained chile and, if desired, the tomato paste. Stir until well mixed. Cook 1 to 2 minutes more. Store in the refrigerator for a week to 10 days, or freeze in small batches.

MAKES ABOUT 3 CUPS

Kitchen Wisdom

Guylyn often skips boiling the chiles. She simply washes them well and then proceeds to purée them with warm water. Of course, the chiles have been hanging around drying on someone's roof so she finishes them off with a little longer boil. In addition to following traditional recipes for enchiladas, the Nusoms have found many new uses for red chile sauce. Add it to fat-free yogurt to make a dip or dressing. A little bit of red chile sauce in a Chinese stir-fry is also a tasty addition.

Recipe Rescuers Guylyn and Lynn Nusom

"What's that movie? The one where she says, 'Life is a banquet and most poor suckers are starving to death,'" shouts Guylyn as she guns the accelerator.

"*Auntie Mame*," I respond, trying not to gasp. Life's banquet is serving me a trip up a significant incline on a rocky New Mexican dirt road in a golf cart festooned with fabric tassels straight out of the Casbah.

"And her husband died falling off a mountain top," I add—envisioning the return trip down the hill. I was clearly in no danger of starving to death, but began to consider the possibility of gravity conspiring to turn me into tossed salad.

This sense of adventure and love for the Southwest infuses the work of Guylyn and Lynn Nusom. For twenty-five years and eleven books, Lynn and his wife have recorded southwestern traditions and recipes. Lynn takes a fanciful look at a legend in the *Billy the Kid Cook Book* and manages to find over 100 ways to use tequila as an ingredient in *The Tequila Cook Book*.

An East Coast transplant who settled in New Mexico when he married Guylyn, Lynn is a food writer who has written extensively about the foods of his adopted home. His lanky frame adapts well to jeans and cowboy hats and he can hold his own at the S Bar X Saloon where a Friday night might find as many horses inside as customers.

Guylyn, who is just as comfortable doing her work in the DAR (Daughters of the American Revolution) as she is decorating old golf carts with a tassel collection, is a third-generation native. She created the concept for the couple's books on local Christmas customs. For those who think only of Christmas as snow-laden, you'll want to trade that gray, melted slush for the colorful parade of Las Posadas, a reenactment of the sojourn of Joseph and Mary, or the simple beauty of the luminarias outlining an adobe roof.

If nothing else, make a bowl of Posole (page 21), a traditional holiday dish found on nearly every New Mexican table. Trying new foods might seem intimidating, but everyone needs to climb an occasional hill in a tasseled golf cart and dish up life's banquet.

Parker House Rolls

$\mathcal{I}$was surprised to discover how many stories and versions of these little rolls there are. Some people claim they were the result of a mistake, some say a rivalry between chefs. In some places I read they were beloved for their soft, chewy exterior while others cite the rolls' crisp crust as the claim to fame. They are still made in the Parker House Hotel in Boston over 100 years after their introduction, and there are many recipes in print. However you make the dough, a Parker House roll gets its distinguishing pocket-book shape from the way you fold it. It is an indisputable fact that the packaged store-bought version of these rolls can't hold a candle to the homemade version.

one recipe Easy Yeast Dough (page 73)

3 tablespoons butter, melted

Divide the yeast dough in half, cover it, and give it a second rising in the refrigerator for about 2 to 3 hours. Reserve one-half for another use (see Note on the next page).

Preheat oven to 400° F.

Roll dough about ½ inch thick. Cut into rounds with a 2½-inch cutter. Work quickly to re-roll the scraps.

Brush the tops of the rounds with some of the butter and make a crease by pressing a chopstick or a clean pencil on the dough, slightly to the right of center. Fold dough along the crease so that the top slightly overlaps the bottom and pinch well to seal. Arrange rolls on a baking sheet so that they are just barely touching. Brush tops with remaining butter and let rise for about 15 minutes.

Bake for 15 to 20 minutes or until the rolls are browned.

MAKES ABOUT 16 ROLLS

Note: This recipe uses half the dough. You may use all of the dough to make a double batch (32 rolls). Or follow directions for Brown-and-Serve Rolls (page 75) or Sticky Buns (page 90).

Georgia Pecan Pie

$\mathcal{M}$y brother-in-law married into this old southern family recipe, thus proving my theory that romance and gastronomy are never too far removed. I was emphatically instructed that the butter should be melted in a cast-iron pan. The first time I tasted this pie it was made with Georgia pecans from the tree in the cow pasture—a well-fertilized tree that gave forth abundantly. The pie was absolutely delicious, so be sure to use good-quality whole pecans when making yours.

I love cast-iron pans, and the older the better. Properly cared for, a good cast-iron pan is virtually nonstick and can be used for just about any task. I never let my pans soak in water, nor do I use soap. A good scrubbing with kosher salt and a quick dry on a burner will keep your pan well seasoned. Seasoning a pan used to be a lesson in patience and was done over time. Nowadays you can purchase your cast iron already seasoned and be instantly gratified.

6 tablespoons butter	1¼ cups light corn syrup
¾ cup sugar	1 recipe Marie Dugan's Pie Crust
4 large eggs	(page 83), or your favorite pie
2 cups whole pecans (or mostly whole)	crust

Preheat oven to 375° F.

Melt butter in a skillet until light brown. Remove from the heat and immediately stir in sugar. Let cool slightly.

Add eggs one at a time, beating after each addition. Add pecans and corn syrup. Line a 9-inch pie pan with 1 round of unbaked pie crust and pour in filling. Bake for 30 to 35 minutes or until just firm and brown. Do not overbake.

MAKES 1 9-INCH PIE

Gingersnap Crumb Crust

When did Brazil nuts go out of fashion? Today you might find a lonely Brazil nut or two in a can of mixed nuts, but throughout my childhood I recall the exotic nut appearing in everything from candy bars and Jell-O salads to this pie crust. Trust me, the pie crust is better than the Jell-O!

1⅓ cups gingersnap crumbs (about 24 1½-inch cookies)

½ cup finely chopped Brazil nuts

4 tablespoons butter, melted

Preheat oven to 375° F.

Mix ingredients well and press into a 9-inch pie pan.

Bake for 8 to 10 minutes. Let cool completely.

MAKES 1 9-INCH PIE CRUST

Cream Pumpkin Pie

The biggest challenge of Thanksgiving dinner is always oven space. This clever pie is cooked on the stove top and refrigerated. You could use any pie crust for the shell, but I find the nutty crumb crust is a perfect contrast to the pudding consistency. If you are so inclined, you may use fat-free evaporated milk and free up a few calories in addition to oven space.

1 recipe Gingersnap Crumb Crust
  (page 30)
1 cup sugar
2 tablespoons arrowroot or
  cornstarch
$\frac{1}{2}$ teaspoon cinnamon
$\frac{1}{2}$ teaspoon nutmeg

$\frac{1}{8}$ teaspoon salt
1 12-ounce can evaporated milk
  (about 1$\frac{1}{2}$ cups)
2 eggs, beaten
3 tablespoons rum or $\frac{3}{4}$ teaspoon
  rum extract
1 15-ounce can cooked pumpkin

Make the crust as directed. Set aside.

In a medium saucepan, mix together sugar, arrowroot, cinnamon, nutmeg, and salt.

In a bowl, blend milk, eggs, and rum together and gradually add to the sugar mixture. Stir well and cook over medium heat, whisking constantly until it starts to boil.

Remove from the heat and add pumpkin. Return the saucepan to the heat, stirring constantly, until ingredients are well incorporated and mixture returns to a boil. Continue stirring and simmer 3 to 5 minutes, or until the pumpkin is a thick pudding.

Fill pie shell. Cool slightly and refrigerate until thoroughly chilled—
about 3 to 4 hours. Serve with whipped cream.

MAKES 8 SLICES

Kitchen Wisdom

Arrowroot, while somewhat more expensive, makes a better thickener
than cornstarch. It has a much cleaner taste and is colorless when cooked.
It must be mixed with a cold liquid before it is added to anything hot.

Buttermilk Pie

I've seen this pie making a reappearance lately. It was a family favorite of ours. The name may dissuade some from trying it, which is unfortunate. It tastes more like a cheesecake than one would first imagine.

2 eggs

1 cup sugar

1 cup buttermilk

1 stick (4 ounces) butter, melted

2 tablespoons flour

1 teaspoon vanilla extract

1 recipe Marie Dugan's Pie Crust
 (page 83), or your favorite pie crust

freshly grated nutmeg, for garnish
 (optional)

Preheat oven to 350° F.

In a large bowl, beat eggs until smooth. Add sugar, buttermilk, butter, flour, and vanilla and mix well.

Line a 9-inch pie pan with 1 round of unbaked pie crust and pour in filling. Sprinkle with a little nutmeg, if desired. Bake for 40 to 45 minutes, or until just firm.

MAKES 1 9-INCH PIE

Kitchen Wisdom

Buttermilk pie is very much like a chess pie and should never be over-cooked. How to tell if it is done? The filling should be set, but not so firm that a little jiggle won't show some movement in the center.

Nashville House Fried Biscuits

*M*y mother-in-law would often reminisce about her birthplace of Brown County, in southern Indiana. It's a quiet community filled with back country roads crowned with covered bridges and an invitation to wander aimlessly. Mom has passed away, but she would often talk about Nashville House fried biscuits. The Nashville House is a restaurant and inn in Nashville, Indiana, and dates back to the mid-19th century. People would come from miles around for the signature fried biscuits and apple butter. On a whim, I called and discovered The Nashville House is still in existence and has been run by the same family since 1927. They kindly allowed me to include their biscuit recipe here. Serve them with Crockpot Apple Butter (page 55).

1 tablespoon plus one teaspoon active dry yeast	1 teaspoon salt
¼ cup warm water	about 5 cups flour
2 cups milk	¼ cup shortening
2 tablespoons sugar	oil, for frying

In a small bowl, add yeast to warm water and blend. Add milk and sugar to yeast and mix well. Set aside.

In a large bowl, blend salt with 3½ cups flour. Cut in shortening and mix well. Add yeast mixture and mix well. Add more flour ½ cup at a time until the dough comes together and is slightly sticky. Set aside in a warm spot until doubled in bulk, about 1 hour.

Punch down dough and roll out to ½ inch thick. Cut into rounds with a 2-inch floured biscuit cutter, reworking the dough as you go. Set aside to rise—about the time it takes for the oil to heat. If they rise too much they will deflate when fried.

Meanwhile, heat oil to 375° F (follow manufacturer's directions for your appliance or see page 185 for deep-frying instructions). Add several biscuits at a time—depending on the size of your cooking vessel. Fry the biscuits until golden brown on each side, about 1 to 2 minutes.

Drain and serve warm.

MAKES ABOUT 3 DOZEN BISCUITS

Kitchen Wisdom

When deep frying, never add too many biscuits at once or the temperature of the oil will drop. Also, you won't be able to cook and retrieve the biscuits in good order.

This recipe is easily doubled and the biscuits can be frozen after frying. Thaw and reheat in a 350° F oven for eight to ten minutes or until biscuits are warmed through and crisp.

Potato Doughnuts

When my friend and neighbor sampled my doughnuts, he proclaimed them good—but not as good as his mom's potato doughnuts. As it turns out, his adoration of these doughnuts is based on more than filial love. And fortunately for us all, Phyllis Sutts shared her recipe and her secrets for success. The dough is a little tricky to work with but worth the effort, yielding doughnuts that are almost as light as air. Phyllis made these to use up leftover mashed potatoes, but you can use prepared and packaged mashed potatoes just as reliably (although these doughnuts are one good reason to make a big pot of mashed potatoes for Sunday supper).

6 cups flour	2¼ cups sugar
1 tablespoon plus 1 teaspoon baking powder	6 tablespoons shortening, melted
1½ teaspoons nutmeg	1½ cups mashed potatoes
1 teaspoon salt	¾ cup milk
3 eggs	oil, for frying

In a large bowl, sift flour with baking powder, nutmeg, and salt. Set aside.

In a separate bowl, beat eggs. Add sugar and continue beating until well mixed. Beat in shortening then potatoes. Mix in milk.

Slowly add dry ingredients and mix until flour just disappears. Cover dough and refrigerate—overnight is best.

Place one third of the dough on a floured surface. Sprinkle dough lightly with flour and roll out ½ inch thick. Cut with a floured doughnut cutter. Set on a tray that has been lightly floured and continue cutting the rest of the doughnuts. Rework and roll out the dough as needed.

Meanwhile, heat oil to 375° F (follow manufacturer's directions for your appliance or see page 185 for deep-frying instructions). Without crowding the pot, fry several doughnuts at once, turning after 1 minute. Cook about another 2 minutes, turning one more time.

If desired, sprinkle doughnuts with confectioners' sugar or cinnamon sugar.

MAKES ABOUT 4 DOZEN 3 ⅓-INCH DOUGHNUTS

Kitchen Wisdom

Phyllis Sutts says the less flour you use, the more tender the doughnuts, but you don't want them to stick all over the rolling pin either. Keeping the cut doughnuts in the refrigerator makes them easier to handle.

FROM THE GARDEN

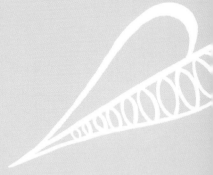

*D*on Juan, Baltimore Belle, Bewitched, Grand Duchess—the names jump off the pages of a rose catalogue with the romance of a Barbara Cartland novel. For me, these names take me back to my early childhood in my yard with 250 rosebushes. Growing roses was my father's passionate hobby. At the time, I considered such flora as quite ordinary. It was no more unique than the wild Queen Anne's lace and blackberries consuming the vacant lot across the street.

My father spent his spare time pruning, spraying, weeding, and watering. I quickly discovered beauty may be skin deep—and a rose's thorn was piercing to the flesh. At least the wild blackberries yielded a luscious treat for the bramble scratches. Is there a taste as sweet for a child, weary with play, as a warm berry plucked on a hot summer afternoon?

I entered the rose garden, on the other hand, only when necessary to earn my weekly allowance scooping the lethal Japanese beetles off rose leaves and putting them into a quart-size pickle jar containing a dollop of gasoline. As I recall, the going rate was twenty-five cents for about a half-quart.

One year I decided I wanted a vegetable garden. I'm not certain how that desire was flamed, unless I had outgrown the endless mud pies I spent hours creating and craved more reward for my earthy culinary efforts. There was a small patch of land that had already been cleared of sod and garnered full sun. Prime real estate in the scheme of a massive rose garden, but I got my way as long as I promised to take care of it.

Ah, the lessons of the garden. Gardening demands patience and is hard work. Once I learned that a carrot seed I planted wasn't producing a carrot after two days in the ground, I had to face the reality that weeds, in fact, matured overnight.

By mid-summer my enthusiasm for gardening had waned considerably. My vision of a larder full of succulent vegetables produced by my own hands was clouded by the sight of hard work as the weeds continually sprouted back-breaking labor.

Still, I managed a small harvest from my vegetable garden, despite the massive neglect I heaped on it and the singular attention the rabbits heaped on it. Radishes were my forte—bright, succulent orbs so juicy they would split at the mere sight of a knife, and were best eaten washed on the spot and salted from a shaker carried in my back pocket. That year I developed a taste for radish tea sandwiches thick with butter which remains with me to this day (although the Wonder Bread has given way to pumpernickel).

I didn't have a garden again until I was an adult. I had finally found an affordable apartment in a small New Jersey town from which I commuted to New York City. There was enough turf between the paved parking space and my door to accommodate two tomato plants and a basil plant, as well as a couple of snap dragons and dahlias to satisfy my now developed appreciation of bloom.

Where rabbits had once ravished my garden, I discovered vermin of the two legged sort. Every time I would just get a tomato to the verge of the perfect stage of ripeness, I would come home to find it plucked clean away by some passer-by. What was once mine had become the community garden for every Tom, Dick, and Harry with some business in the office above my apartment.

Every garden has its seasons and so does every gardener. My next endeavor was as a new mother in my first house. I became an herb gardener and went at it with the same intensity my father had with his roses. My son discovered his playground shrinking with each passing year as I added more footage to my herb garden. He and his sister earned spending money picking weeds. Going rate was about fifty cents a half-peck box, adjusting for inflation.

By now I was a full-fledged foodie and saw the garden as an extension of my kitchen. I didn't just grow basil, I grew seven varieties of *Ocimum basilicum:* sweet, bush, camphor, holy, lemon, leaf, and purple. If there were an *O. basilicum* to be had, I had it.

I made vinegars from home grown chive blossoms, nasturtium flowers, purple basil, tarragon, and burnet. I candied angelica and borage. I grew sesame seeds (pretty, but you'd need at least a quarter acre to get enough to seed a loaf of bread).

I discovered feverfew tea for a headache tonic and chamomile as a sleep aid. I cooked with three varieties of sage and five of mint.

I've tended vegetable gardens just as extensive as the herb garden—my patience expanding to accommodate the several-year wait for a decent asparagus patch and my palate swelling to enjoy freshly picked okra, eggplant, and Brussels sprouts. Now that the weed-picking, beetle-snuffing kids are gone and we've traded acreage for city life, I've scaled the garden back to several containers and a twelve-by-two-by-three foot raised bed. A bonus is that I don't have to weed on my aging knees.

Whatever I don't grow, I get from my subscription to a CSA (community supported agriculture). With a CSA, every spring I buy a share in a farm and get a weekly delivery of fabulous produce ranging from spring garlic to just-picked apples. There are beets and parsnips for the borscht and berries for the pies.

Here's all I need to grow to meet my kitchen needs: purple basil, sweet basil, and holy basil (wonderful for Thai stir-fry) in a large container; a cherry tomato plant in a container; one heirloom tomato and one beefsteak tomato plant in the bed; sugar snap peas in a box to climb up the fence in early spring; tarragon, sage, chives, and chervil to fill in the bed. And, of course, one floribunda climbing rose bush.

Whether they come from your garden or not, the fresh produce in these recipes celebrate the peak of the season.

The Rev's Okra

$\mathcal{M}$y favorite place to hang out in my neighborhood is the corner newsstand where the gossip in the air is more interesting than what's on the printed page. My hound is most happy when the Rev is there to scratch her ears. When the Rev is not preaching the word, our many recipe exchanges have proven he's also a pretty good cook. One of sixteen children growing up in South Carolina, he says, "I just learned how to cook because that's what you had to do."

I'm glad he did and you will be, too, when you taste this dish. The Rev says it's best served over Carolina rice. His secret is to just barely steam the okra on top of the other vegetables and never wash the okra after it has been cut.

These are approximate proportions and can be adapted to what's on hand. Go ahead and substitute frozen for any ingredient except the okra.

2 cups corn	⅛ teaspoon dried thyme
1 cup lima beans	salt and pepper to taste
1 or 2 tomatoes, peeled, seeded, and chopped (about 1 cup)	24 to 30 fresh okra pods

In a large sauté pan, mix corn, lima beans, tomatoes, thyme, salt, and pepper. Simmer, covered, until almost tender, about 10 minutes depending on the freshness of your ingredients. Add a little water if there is not much liquid.

Meanwhile, wash okra pods and dry completely. Remove the stem end, but keep the tail and cut into ¼-inch rounds.

Place okra rounds on top of the other vegetables, cover, and continue cooking for about 5 minutes or until the okra is just tender and turns a bright green.

MAKES ABOUT 5 CUPS

Carrot Pudding (Gajraila from Pakistan)

*W*hen I taught cooking to the visually impaired, I often went to the student's home. The mother of one of my young charges was from Pakistan and she treated me to an elaborate tea after every lesson. I fell in love with this dish which is akin to carrot cake in flavor. I later learned that it can also be served as a breakfast dish. Since I generally dislike breakfast, I loved this dish even more; I can enjoy breakfast and a vegetable all at once.

1 quart milk

¼ cup basmati or Carolina long-grain rice

1 pound carrots, scrubbed and grated

½ cup sugar (or more, depending on the sweetness of the carrots)

¾ teaspoon ground cardamom

½ cup golden raisins

¼ cup shelled pistachios

Pour milk into a medium saucepan, add rice, and soak for 30 minutes.

Add carrots, sugar, and cardamom and bring mixture to a boil. Reduce heat and simmer, uncovered, for 1½ hours, scraping down the sides of the pan and stirring occasionally to keep rice from sticking to the bottom.

If a thick pudding is desired, mash some of the mixture with a potato masher or immersion blender. Add raisins and taste for sweetness. Add more sugar if desired. Cook 30 minutes longer, stirring every so often to prevent sticking.

When pudding is done, transfer to a 1-quart serving dish or individual ramekins. Refrigerate until thoroughly chilled and garnish with pistachios.

MAKES 3 CUPS

French Onion Dip

*A*lso known as California Dip, I don't think there was a potato chip served in the sixties without this accompaniment. It usually was made with dehydrated soup mix and today you can even find it already prepared in the dairy case. This version is fresher and less cloying than the convenience variety and lends itself to a multitude of adaptations and quick pantry saves. It pairs well with other dips (such as the Green Goddess Dressing on page 46) to make a festive crudité.

1 cup sour cream

2 teaspoons instant beef bouillon granules

2 to 4 tablespoons minced onion, as desired

In a medium bowl, blend ingredients and refrigerate for 2 to 3 hours to allow flavors to develop.

MAKES 1 CUP

Kitchen Wisdom

With a recipe this basic you can add your own innovations: a tablespoon of sherry, finely minced dry mushrooms, or a grating of Gruyère cheese. Substitute leeks or scallions for the onions. Mashed roasted garlic is a fine addition as are ground toasted almonds. If the dip needs more body, add a little cream cheese. Dippers can be anything from common chips to exotic vegetables such as Belgian endive or steamed cardoon.

Green Goddess Dressing

$\mathcal{T}$his is one of the recipes that made all my tasters exclaim, "I remember this! Why did we stop eating this?" Judging from that response you'd think the name derived from the taste. In actuality, the dressing was created in San Francisco in the early 1900s to honor an actor in a play called *The Green Goddess*. It's a versatile dressing and also makes a delicious dip for vegetables and shellfish. On a salad, I'm partial to fresh Bibb lettuce or romaine with avocado slices. Although it has nothing Irish about it, I'll often serve it on St. Patrick's Day because of its natural color.

1 cup parsley, washed, dried, most of the stems removed

1 clove garlic, crushed

1 scallion, cut into 1-inch pieces

2 tablespoons tarragon vinegar

1 teaspoon Dijon mustard

1 teaspoon anchovy paste (or more, if desired)

1 cup mayonnaise

1 cup sour cream

In a food processor or blender, combine parsley, garlic, scallion, vinegar, mustard, and anchovy paste until vegetables are minced. Add mayonnaise and sour cream and blend well. Refrigerate for several hours or overnight to develop flavors. Use within 5 to 7 days.

MAKES ABOUT 2 1/4 CUPS

Pensacola Gaspachee Salad

This salad is peculiar to the Pensacola region of Florida. I've seen it spelled several ways and made with either a mayonnaise-based dressing or oil and vinegar. I like the mayonnaise dressing but add a splash of vinegar for a little tang. One ingredient is indisputable: hardtack or Crown Pilot crackers. The vegetables tend to get weepy if salted ahead of time, so serve this with a salt shaker on the table if that's your preference.

8 Crown Pilot crackers (one sleeve, 4.6 ounces) or 5 ounces hardtack

¾ cup mayonnaise

1 tablespoon cider vinegar

black pepper to taste

3 stalks celery, diced ¼ inch

2 cucumbers, peeled, seeded, and diced ¼ inch

2 large tomatoes, chopped

1 green bell pepper, seeded, membrane removed, and diced ¼ inch

1 medium Spanish onion, diced ¼ inch

Bibb lettuce, for serving

Soak crackers in water for about 1 hour, until completely soft. Squeeze dry. There should be about 1 cup.

Mix crackers, mayonnaise, vinegar, and pepper together. Toss with celery, cucumbers, tomatoes, bell pepper, and onion and serve well chilled on lettuce.

MAKES 8 CUPS

Borscht

*W*hile this soup is commonly known, it is rarely made from scratch at home. I'm always looking for international recipes and someone who can teach me how to make them as authentically as possible. In this case I used three techniques for rescuing recipes. I found a Russian Orthodox Church celebrating Butter Sunday during Easter and obtained a basic recipe from the church community. Next, a Russian taxicab driver instructed me on the proper way to garnish and serve the soup. Finally, my son spent a summer in St. Petersburg, Russia, and his host family noted that the soup can be made with or without meat. I now have a delicious recipe and made some friends along the way.

Borscht can be served hot or cold. Either way, a good loaf of pumpernickel with butter is a fine addition. This particular recipe makes a lot and can be halved, but it doesn't really cut down on the work. Anyway, another recipe rescuer axiom is to share with friends and neighbors.

¼ cup olive oil

1 large onion, diced (about 1½ cups)

1 carrot, peeled and coarsely grated (about 1 cup)

1 parsnip, peeled and coarsely grated (about 1 cup)

1 pound potatoes, peeled and coarsely grated (about 2 medium potatoes)

2 tablespoons tomato paste

1 tablespoon sugar

2 pounds beets, peeled and coarsely grated (about 2 quarts)

1 pound sauerkraut, rinsed and drained (about 3 cups), plus more for serving

2 quarts water

1 teaspoon salt

¼ teaspoon black pepper

1 teaspoon dried dill or 1 tablespoon chopped fresh dill

for garnish: sour cream, lemon slices, fresh dill sprigs

In a stockpot, heat olive oil; add in onion and sauté until translucent. Add carrot and sauté for about 1 minute. Add parsnip and potatoes and sauté another minute. Add tomato paste and sugar and stir well.

Add beets, 1 pound sauerkraut, water, salt, and pepper. Blend well and bring to a boil. Reduce heat, cover, and simmer for 1½ hours, stirring occasionally. Add the dill and taste the soup. Adjust seasonings if necessary, adding a little more salt or pepper.

To serve, place a tablespoon or two of sauerkraut in the bottom of the bowl, add the soup, and garnish with sour cream, lemon slice, and fresh dill sprig.

MAKES 3 QUARTS
1 QUART = 1 LITER = 32 FL OZ.

Kitchen Wisdom

For a heartier borscht, add a pound or so of beef shin or short rib and simmer an extra hour or so. This is especially good served steamy hot on a cold winter's night.

⸺ •• ⸺

When sauerkraut is an ingredient in a cooked recipe, I prefer to rinse and drain it before adding it to the dish. The flavor is much sweeter. When I'm using kraut as a garnish, I don't drain the juice off because a little bit of the brine adds just enough tang to the soup.

Recipe Rescuer Doug Fincke

Doug Fincke is obsessed by graft. His business partners arrive by stealth and swarm in summer activity. Their business deal begins with chaos theory and the rain forest. A slight change can set off a chain of events with disastrous consequences. Out of the ruins of Eden, he contrives sweetness.

Doug Fincke is a pomologist—an apple grower. He lives, breathes, eats, and even drinks apples. Heirloom apples are his stock in trade. With each passing season he is at the mercy of the weather and bee pollination, as well as the marketplace.

Fincke considers himself a tenant farmer carrying on a two-hundred-year-old tradition. In a unique modern-day arrangement, he manages the orchards at Montgomery Place, a historic estate in the Hudson Valley of New York State. The estate began in 1804 when the Livingston family bought the property from a Dutch apple grower. Fincke lives on the estate with his family in a yellow Victorian cottage set high on a hill overlooking the orchards.

"The old apple varieties are like people," says Doug Fincke. "You get to know all their intrinsic qualities."

Today's apples in the supermarket are a long way from Johnny Appleseed. Pickers find it expedient to pick a tree clean to supply the shippers and produce purveyors. Taste and flavor have given way to other cost-saving concerns. Fincke notes that apples have developed to suit our fast-paced lifestyle with little regard for the taste of the apple. Heirloom apple varieties, on the other hand, can ripen on a tree over the course of three weeks. A picker has to look at each apple and know when to harvest it. For this intimacy you are rewarded.

Says Fincke, "Apples in a supermarket could be a year old due to advanced storage technology. A small farm stand picks the apples over the course of a few weeks so they are always crisp and flavorful."

Golden Russets and Newtown Pippins are his favorites. A Golden Russet is small, dense, and tart. It finds its way into pies and cider for the farmstand and hard cider for his household. The Newtown Pippin is picked after the first of November and isn't much to eat right off the tree, but store it in the garage (Fincke advocates a root cellar) at around forty degrees for a month and it explodes with flavor.

Montgomery Place orchards were "modernized" in the seventies and the older varieties gave way to the commercial varieties of Red Delicious, Golden Delicious, and Rome. Sixteen years ago, Fincke came and decided because the operation was small, he had the time to learn about the old varieties. He has been propagating them ever since and is slowly returning heirlooms to the orchard. The apples are sold at Montgomery Place Orchards farmstand on Route 9 in the scenic hamlet of Annandale-on-Hudson, New York.

Smothered Pork Chops

At Montgomery Place Orchards, this dish is made in November after the farm market business slows and they can take their time to really enjoy a meal. Most often they will have homemade cider made from heirloom apples available, although the bottled commercial product works well. Many families ring in the New Year with pork and sauerkraut for good luck, and this recipe fits the bill for that calendar change, too. I prefer sweeter apples with this such as Braeburn, or even Rome, because it doesn't matter if the apples break down in the cooking. Serve with mashed potatoes or turnips.

4 center-cut pork chops, ¾ inch thick (about 2 pounds)	½ teaspoon dried thyme
2 tablespoons grainy mustard	¼ teaspoon salt
1 tablespoon olive oil	¼ teaspoon black pepper
1 large onion, cut in half lengthwise and thinly sliced crosswise	2 large apples, cored, cut into 8 wedges and then 1-inch pieces
1 12-ounce bottle hard cider (or apple cider)	1 pound sauerkraut, rinsed and drained (about 3 cups drained)

Rub chops evenly with mustard.

Heat oil in a large Dutch oven. Add pork chops (in 2 batches if necessary) and brown on both sides. Set aside. Add onion and sauté until limp. Add cider, stirring to deglaze all the brown bits from the bottom of the pan. Add thyme, salt, and pepper.

Return chops to pan and smother with apples and sauerkraut. Bring to a boil. Then lower heat, cover, and simmer for about 45 minutes or until the chops are tender. Check occasionally during cooking.

MAKES 4 HEARTY SERVINGS

Crockpot Apple Butter

A slow cooker is well-suited to the long, even heat that is required to break down the cell walls of apples and release their juices. The resulting reduction is nature's caramel sauce. The only sugar in this recipe comes naturally from the apples. While it is the definitive accompaniment to Nashville House Fried Biscuits (page 34), it is also fabulous on ice cream or with pork chops. Apple butter freezes well, and in the dead of winter will make even mundane toast a welcome breakfast treat.

5 pounds apples, peeled, cored, and chopped into 1-inch pieces (about 12 cups)

1 teaspoon cinnamon

1 teaspoon cardamom

½ cup apple cider

Mix ingredients together and add to a 3-quart crockpot (slow cooker). Cover and heat on high for 4 hours. Scrape down sides and continue cooking, scraping down sides about every 2 to 3 hours.

After about 10 hours, remove lid and continue cooking another 1 to 2 hours. Stir occasionally. Mixture will become thick and caramel-colored. Apple butter is done when it is reduced by three-quarters and a spoon pulled through the sauce makes a ridge.

MAKES 3 CUPS

Kitchen Wisdom

Of course the quality of the apples is especially important when reducing the fruit this much. You'll want just-picked apples from your local stand. Ask your grower what variety is particularly good this year.

Quince and Apple Pie

*T*here's nothing quite like the combination of quince and apple. It's what I imagine eating a bowl of fragrant roses would be like, but with a better texture. If you can't find quince for this pie, an equal amount of apple slices can be substituted. Seek out an apple farm that sells heirloom apples. You will be glad you did.

1⅔ pounds good baking apples, peeled, cored, and cut into 1-inch chunks (4 cups)

1 pound quince, peeled, cored, and cut into 1-inch chunks (2 cups)

½ cup granulated sugar

½ cup brown sugar

2 tablespoons flour

1 teaspoon cinnamon

½ teaspoon freshly grated nutmeg

1 recipe Marie Dugan's Pie Crust (page 83), or your favorite pie crust

Preheat oven to 400° F.

Combine apples, quince, both sugars, flour, cinnamon, and nutmeg and mix well.

Line a 9-inch pie pan with 1 round of unbaked pie crust and spoon in filling. Top with second round of pie crust and crimp edges. Cut slits to vent steam.

Bake on the bottom rack of the oven for 10 minutes. Reduce oven temperature heat to 350° F degrees and continue baking 40 to 45 minutes more, or until a little juice bubbles from the vents.

MAKES 1 9-INCH PIE

Farmers Market Berry Pie

*H*ere's a recipe for those days when your local farmers market is bejeweled with fresh berries. This recipe works for any berry—including a mix—all you need is to gather four cups worth. Look for blueberries, blackberries, boysenberries, gooseberries, loganberries, raspberries, and strawberries at the peak of the season. Although it will take intense discipline to do this, cool the pie thoroughly before cutting to allow the filling to set up.

STREUSEL TOPPING
⅓ cup butter
⅓ cup brown sugar
¾ cup flour

PIE FILLING
4 cups berries, picked over, thoroughly dried
1⅓ cups sugar
⅓ cup flour

1 recipe Marie Dugan's Pie Crust (page 83), or your favorite pie crust

Preheat oven to 425° F.

Make the streusel topping: With a pastry cutter, blend butter, sugar, and flour together to make coarse crumbs. Set aside.

Make the pie filling: Gently mix berries with sugar and flour.

Assemble and bake the pie: Line a 9-inch pie pan with 1 round of unbaked pie crust and pour in filling. Sprinkle top of pie with streusel topping. Bake for 35 to 45 minutes, or until topping is crisp and there is a little bit of juice bubbling around the edge. Let cool thoroughly.

MAKES ONE 9-INCH PIE

RAINY DAYS

On my dresser there's a photograph of a woman I never met. Her face looks out at me and sometimes—more and more with each passing year—I can see myself. Our connection is food and my grandmother. Aunt Kitten is my great aunt, my mother's mother's sister. She passed away when I was still an infant, but I know her through family stories. These are the stories that are told on a rainy day when nostalgia takes hold. We sip tea, eat toasted brown bread, and savor the conversation.

My family members recall the delight of sitting at Aunt Kitten's table. Plates piled high with potatoes, green beans, and a perfect roast would be passed, passed again, and then again. You didn't just walk away fed, you walked away (or maybe crawled) with a satisfaction that went deeper than your belly. She was known for her canning: fruits that seemed just-picked fresh in the dead of winter; pickles that tickled your tongue; and chow-chow, a sweet-and-sour blend of corn, green pepper, and onions. Long after her only child was grown and gone, Kitten continued to "put foods by" and maintain a massive pantry.

On the day that her husband died, she had just completed a morning of canning. Each jar was polished to show off the colorful contents; a display of beauty and bounty waiting for his return from work. As the mourners gathered, a helpful person suggested putting the jars away. Kitten, with tears in her eyes, said, "I never put them away until he comes home. He so liked to see them; he said they looked like jewels."

This rainy day story is my culinary legacy. I carry it with me along with the cast-iron skillets that belonged to my mother-in-law and my grandmother's wooden spoon. I feel the powerful connection of food and family. The crack in the wooden spoon gave birth to a family joke: it must have been the spoon that kept my Irish grandfather in line. I imagine the cast-iron skillets are seasoned with the spices of my husband's childhood; maybe if I try hard enough I could taste them, perhaps divining a moment in time that wasn't mine.

Rainy days can be a personal holiday: an excuse to retreat from the world with a new book, the binding aching with promise. A time to be unabashedly self-indulgent and have a second piece of peach pie. Or a time to perfume the damp air with the smells of a favorite childhood dish.

While I enjoy rainy days, my son has fond memories of snow days. I counted the closing of his school as a curse and major upheaval in my life, but Ben recalls the delight and opportunity of nature's unexpected gift. A snow day requires us to release all expectation and change our plans. We looked through old family photographs, took one too many trips down the sledding hill, and had one too many helpings of hot chocolate and marshmallows.

Bad weather is a cook's companion. We can justify retreating to the kitchen and spending time taking stock of the larder. Recipes we don't have time to coddle during fair weather can call us to the stove. I wonder how many pots of baked beans have softened a New England storm, while across the world someone chops Korean kimchee to the rhythm of the rain?

Sometimes the storm is an emotional barometer; a day when moods or life events take over. At these times comfort can be elusive. The act of kneading bread dough or slicing vegetables mindlessly is just what is called for. The repetitive activity is like a meditation and nurtures us more than food. On these "rainy" afternoons I make dinner rolls and pie crust to set aside in the freezer for better days.

These recipes require some time, or at the very least, a watchful eye for longer cook times and a hand for an occasional stir. This makes them perfect for the days when bad weather keeps us from routine and gives us time in the kitchen.

Freezer Pickles

*H*ome canning used to be as common as sliced bread. Today, it seems like an ancient art that is fraught with big equipment, hard work, and potential danger. Imagine my delight when I discovered a recipe for "putting by" homemade pickles without the hassle of canning. I love these bread and butter pickles with just the right amount of sweet, sour, and crunch. It's so easy to do a batch here and a batch there. Suddenly you have a nice winter stash. I find the three cup plastic salad and soup containers are ideal for storage because they can be easily stacked. Serve this with Barbecue Ham Sandwich (page 104).

2 quarts kirby cucumbers (about 2 pounds), washed well and sliced into ¼-quarter inch rounds	2 cups sugar
	1 cup cider vinegar
	3 bay leaves
1 medium onion, thinly sliced	2 tablespoons celery seeds
2 tablespoons kosher salt	1½ tablespoons mustard seeds

Mix cucumbers, onion, and salt in a 2½-quart glass heat resistant bowl. Set aside.

In a medium saucepan, heat sugar, vinegar, bay leaves, celery seeds, and mustard seeds just to boiling, stirring constantly until sugar is dissolved. Pour sugar mixture over cucumbers and let stand overnight or for 24 hours.

Leaving 1 inch head space, pack in freezable containers, making sure the pickles are covered in juice. Check to make sure the cover is tightly sealed; freeze.

It is best to use the pickles within 3 months. To thaw, place in the refrigerator for about 24 hours. Serve cold. Thawed pickles will keep for up to 1 week in the refrigerator.

MAKES ABOUT 4 CUPS PICKLES, DRAINED

Kitchen Wisdom

Kirby cucumbers are a variety that is ideal for pickling. They always come unwaxed and their compact size (about three to six inches) makes a nice pickle. They can be a little bitter at the ends, so be sure to trim about one-quarter inch off each end. Kirbys are available year-long, but are best when purchased locally from a farm stand at the peak of summer's bounty.

Kimchee

*M*rs. Knapp came to this country from Korea as a young woman. Every fall she continues the tradition of making kimchee. All the mothers, daughters, and grandmothers gather together to make a big supply to last the winter. There are many different kinds of kimchee and there are regional preferences. I always found kimchee to be too strong in flavor, but Mrs. Knapp's is the perfect blend of salty, hot, and spicy tastes with the crunchy texture of the cabbage. Serve this as you would any pickle or add some to a stir-fry. A spoonful is particularly good when you have a winter head-cold.

1 2- to 2½-pound napa cabbage

3 tablespoons kosher salt

1 Korean radish (called "moo" or "mooshi"), optional

1 to 2 tablespoons coarsely ground Korean chile pepper, or crushed red pepper

½ cup chopped scallions (about 6)

1 tablespoon minced peeled fresh ginger (about 1 inch)

2 cloves garlic, minced (about 1 tablespoon)

½ teaspoon MSG, optional

1 to 3 teaspoons coarse sea salt

1 cup water

Trim bottom from cabbage. Quarter lengthwise and then slice crosswise into 1-inch pieces. Rinse and place in a large bowl with some of the water still clinging to the leaves. Sprinkle with kosher salt and mix well. Set aside for 2 to 3 hours or until wilted. Drain and rinse well.

If using Korean radish, peel and slice into 1-inch pieces. Toss with chile pepper. Add cabbage, scallions, ginger, garlic, and MSG. Season with salt to taste. The cabbage should be crunchy and salty like a pickle. Adjust seasoning and add water. Toss cabbage and mix well.

Scoop kimchee into clean glass jars. Press down after each addition so that the mixture is firmly packed into the jar. Pour the liquid into the jars. The cabbage should be mostly covered by the liquid. Store in refrigerator as you would any pickled item.

MAKES ABOUT 6 CUPS

Kitchen Wisdom

Mrs. Knapp suggests omitting the radish if you cannot find the Korean variety (it looks like portly daikon radish, just a little more rounded and compact). You can substitute a daikon but it will not have the same crisp texture of the Korean radish. Both the radish and coarsely ground Korean chile pepper are available at Korean markets. The Korean chile pepper tends to be a little sweeter than other chiles and adds a nice color to the kimchee.

Breakfast Sausage

"*H*og butcherin' time" took place in the winter when the cold temperature assured the meat would be thoroughly chilled. It was a community event with neighbors helping each other and is still practiced today in some parts of the country. Sausage making was an integral part of the process to avoid any waste. Today we grab prepared sausage from the supermarket shelves. I was once asked by someone on a strict diet due to allergies if there was a sausage product without additives. I did some research and testing and discovered how simple it is to make your own. Whether you have allergies or not, the taste is much fresher. It's also fun experimenting to make the sausage hotter or sweeter.

1½ teaspoons brown sugar

1 teaspoon dried sage, crumbled

1 teaspoon salt

½ teaspoon black pepper

½ teaspoon sweet paprika

⅛ teaspoon crushed red pepper

1 pound freshly ground pork

1 tablespoon ice water

vegetable oil, for frying

In a small bowl, mix brown sugar, sage, salt, black pepper, paprika, and red pepper. Toss on top of the ground pork and sprinkle with ice water. Knead, mixing the seasoning evenly throughout the meat.

Form the meat into patties. Fry in a skillet with a small amount of oil until the center is no longer pink or freeze for future use. Thaw overnight in the refrigerator before cooking.

MAKES 1 POUND BULK SAUSAGE, OR ABOUT 1 DOZEN PATTIES

Kitchen Wisdom

I have a terrific butcher whom I ask to grind my pork when I order it so that it is absolutely fresh and well-trimmed of extra fat. You may do the same at home with any pork butt. Trim away fat and either grind the pork in a meat grinder or process in a food processor until coarsely ground like hamburger.

———— •• ————

Dipping your hands in a bowl of ice water as you knead the meat will keep it from sticking to your hands.

Chiles Rellenos

*R*ecipe rescuer Lynn Nusom gave me this recipe, and he told me that chiles rellenos literally means "stuffed chiles." This is one of those authentic southwestern recipes that comes from the blending of Mexican and Spanish influences. It used to be in every Mom and Pop eatery along the roadside, but now is being replaced with a pale imitation, a prepackaged frozen version. Rellenos are labor intensive, but the resulting blend of melted cheese, hot pepper, and crunch is worth the work. Lynn says it's fine to add shrimp, ground pork, or other ingredients to give it your personal touch.

8 long, mild green chiles	½ teaspoon salt
8 pieces of mild cheese, such as	½ teaspoon ground cumin
longhorn, cut slightly smaller than	⅛ teaspoon cayenne pepper, or to
the chiles	taste
½ cup flour	3 eggs, beaten
½ teaspoon garlic powder	oil, for frying
½ teaspoon baking soda	

Roast the chiles over a gas flame or electric burner until the skin blisters. Place them in a paper bag and steam them until the skin is loosened. Peel, keeping the stem intact.

Slit the chiles in half lengthwise, being careful not to cut the top or bottom. Remove the seeds and place a piece of cheese inside each chile. Make a tight seal by folding one edge over the other. Set aside.

Mix flour, garlic powder, baking soda, salt, cumin, and pepper together. Dip the chiles into the beaten egg, then coat with flour mixture, then dip into the egg again.

Meanwhile, heat oil to 375° F in a deep fryer or large heavy pot (follow manufacturer's directions for your appliance or see page 185 for deep-frying instructions). Deep-fry the chiles until golden brown. Drain and serve immediately.

SERVES 4 TO 6

Kitchen Wisdom

Lynn says long green New Mexico chiles are best for stuffing, but Anaheim and poblano chiles also work well and are easier to find. He says chiles rellenos are traditionally served with red rice and refried beans. For more information about New Mexican ingredients, read Lynn Nusom's *New Mexico Cook Book.*

Genuine Boston Baked Beans

I still can't find baked beans as good as my grandmother's, but this comes a close second. I have old cookbooks that use leftover baked beans in a variety of ways. Mixed with an egg and coated with cracker crumbs it makes a fine croquette. There are recipes calling for baked beans in tomato soup, and I personally have enjoyed a baked bean sandwich on hearty rye bread. Traditionally, Boston baked beans are paired with steamed Boston Brown Bread (page 72).

1 pound pea beans, picked over and rinsed

1 onion, quartered

3 tablespoons dark brown sugar

1 tablespoon dry mustard

½ cup dark molasses

¼ pound salt pork, diced

In a large Dutch oven or bean pot, combine beans and enough water to cover and bring to a boil. Reduce heat, cover pot, and simmer for 30 to 45 minutes. Drain.

Preheat oven to 250° F.

Return beans to Dutch oven. Cover with fresh water. Add onion, brown sugar, mustard, molasses, and salt pork and mix well. Bring to a boil. Remove from heat, cover, and bake in the oven for at least 5 hours. Check occasionally and add more water if drying out.

Uncover. Stir well. Continue baking uncovered 1 to 2 hours. Stir every once in a while to give beans an even mahogany color. Again, add a little more water if the beans begin to dry.

MAKES ABOUT 5 CUPS

Boston Brown Bread

As a little girl, I remember eating rounds of brown bread with a raisin cream cheese spread. This healthful bread is so easy to make and lends itself to any dried fruit addition—raisins, cherries, plums, or cranberries. Traditionally, this bread is served with Boston Baked Beans (page 70). This could also be made in a slow cooker by increasing cooking to four to six hours on a high setting. You'll also need a mold that comfortably fits your style of slow cooker and accommodates the water.

1 cup yellow cornmeal	1 teaspoon salt
1 cup rye flour	¾ cup molasses
1 cup graham or whole wheat flour	1½ cups buttermilk
1 teaspoon baking soda	

Grease 2 10- to 16-ounce coffee cans or molds. Set aside. Place a rack in the bottom of a kettle large enough to hold the molds.

In a large bowl, sift together the cornmeal, flours, baking soda, and salt. Stir in molasses and buttermilk and mix well.

Fill the molds two-thirds full, cover with lids or foil, and place on the rack in the kettle. Add hot water halfway up the side of the molds. Cover and heat to boiling. Reduce heat and simmer for 2 to 3 hours or until the breads are firm to the touch and a long skewer inserted into the middle comes out clean. Check the water level occasionally to keep at the halfway mark.

Let the breads cool. Unmold by running a knife around the breads. If the bread is stubborn, invert and give it a few good shakes.

MAKES 2 LOAVES, OR ABOUT 12 SLICES

Easy Yeast Dough

When I was fresh out of college and in my first real job I shared an apartment with another graduate, Carol Ganotis. Her mother, Betty Rees, made rolls with this dough. She took them to almost every church supper as well as the weekly family dinner gathering—not to mention the care packages she made for us. When she gave me the recipe she was emphatic that the second addition of flour must be stirred in with a wooden spoon. I must admit to cheating once or twice and using a heavy-duty mixer and being disappointed in the result. Mom always does know best. This is a very versatile dough and adapts well to many uses.

2 cups lukewarm water (105° F to 115° F)	2 tablespoons butter, cut in pieces
2 ¼-ounce envelopes active dry yeast	1 tablespoon plus 1 teaspoon salt
¼ cup sugar	2 eggs, beaten
	about 7 cups bread flour

In a small bowl, combine ½ cup water and yeast.

In a separate mixing bowl, add sugar, butter, and salt to remaining 1½ cups water. Stir to melt butter and blend ingredients. Add yeast mixture and eggs and mix well.

Using an electric mixer, beat together 2 cups flour with yeast mixture. Add 3 more cups flour, a handful at a time, stirring with a wooden spoon. Dough will be sticky.

Knead dough for 10 minutes, adding 1½ to 2 cups more flour, ¼ cup at a time, until the dough is smooth and elastic.

Place dough in a greased bowl. Cover and set aside to rise in a warm spot until doubled in bulk, about 1 hour.

Punch down dough and knead several more times. Follow directions for Parker House Rolls (page 27), Brown-and-Serve Rolls (page 75), Sticky Buns (page 90), or recipe of your choice.

Kitchen Wisdom

Place your dough in a greased two-quart glass liquid measure to rise. Make a note of the volume of dough. It will be easy to tell when it has doubled in bulk.

Brown–and–Serve Rolls

These are so easy to make ahead for holidays. But don't save them just for a special occasion—homemade bread and soup in the freezer is like a rainy-day savings account. You'll have a wonderful meal on a hectic night with virtually no effort.

1 recipe Easy Yeast Dough (page 73)

Preheat oven to 275° F.

Divide dough in half. With each half form 12 balls and set in rows in an 8-inch square pan. Cover and let rise until doubled in bulk, about 30 minutes.

Bake rolls for 25 to 30 minutes, or until cooked through but not brown. Transfer to racks to cool. Place in gallon freezer bags and store in refrigerator for use within 1 to 2 days. Or freeze for up to 2 to 3 months. To serve, thaw frozen rolls to room temperature. Preheat oven to 400° F. Place rolls on a baking sheet. Bake 8 to 10 minutes, or until browned. Pull apart and serve immediately.

If serving right away: Remove rolls from 275° F oven. Preheat oven to 400° F. Bake rolls for 8 to 10 minutes until golden brown. Pull apart and serve immediately.

MAKES 24 ROLLS

Zahtar

While researching recipes, I met a terrific home cook named Helen Hamaty. She introduced me to Lebanese cooking and this wonderful spice mix. Zahtar is used most often to season breads, but it also seasons salads and vegetables. Helen mixes a little zahtar with olive oil as a condiment for pita bread. You can buy it in Middle Eastern stores or online (see page 187), or you can make your own mix, as follows.

¼ cup ground sumac

3 tablespoons ground thyme

1 tablespoon ground marjoram

3 tablespoons toasted sesame seeds

½ teaspoon salt, or to taste

Mix all ingredients in a small bowl. Store in an airtight container.

MAKES ABOUT ½ CUP

Kitchen Wisdom

Sumac is a berry from a bush that grows wild in the Middle East. (Note: North American sumac is poisonous.) It has an astringent, lemony taste and the zest of a lemon is sometimes used as a substitute. Look for sumac in Middle Eastern stores or online (see page 187). Some ground sumac can be quite salty, so adjust your recipes accordingly.

Recipe Rescuers Fred and Jeanne Sach

"Do you think he will have made a pie?" my husband, Bill, asks urgently.

"I don't know," I respond, eyes glued to the map.

We are winding our way through a series of interstate highways in search of what has been billed as the most incredible peach pie recipe. I'm more concerned about not driving into oblivion than I am about having a snack.

As is usually the case, the peach pie is discovered in casual conversation. Bill mentions to a colleague that I'm working on this book and he discovers her father makes a perfect peach pie. Suddenly I have to drop everything. My internal compass is set on peach pie.

We drive into an older development and find ourselves in front of a cheerful place with tomato plants growing in the yard and a large evergreen nearly as big as the house. I instinctively know that the tree grew with the kids and that this is a gardener who plants according to sun rather than convention. My instinct also tells me there is peach pie inside and that the long drive will have been worth it.

Fred is a retired teacher and the Sachs often hosted faculty parties. They are true recipe rescuers. Jeanne hands me a stack of recipes that have been carefully recorded, copied, and distributed to family members around the country. The recipes vary—from the hoped-for peach pie to a venison chili Fred's late brother was known for making.

Viola's Kentucky Peach Pie (page 79) originated with Fred's grandmother in Athertonville, Kentucky. Fred recalls visiting his grandmother's small house where the cooking was done on a wood stove. The pie is straight-ahead simple (peaches, sugar, eggs, vanilla), yet the result is deceptive. Plump, curvaceous peaches yield to a sauce so creamy, tasters can't believe there is no custard in the pie. Success, of course, lies in just-picked peaches from a local farm stand.

"There's something about picking them yourself and making your own fruit pie," says Jeanne who also picks thirty pounds of blueberries every summer to freeze for winter pies. The peach pie, though, must be made in season with fresh peaches and enjoyed often, though briefly.

Fred comes out of the kitchen, peach pie in hand. It is as wonderful as everyone said it would be. As a matter of fact, it is the best peach pie—no, maybe even the best pie—I have ever eaten.

If a recipe were a roadmap, Viola's Kentucky Peach Pie would be a cartographer's dream. What if Fred had lost this recipe? We would be left with ordinary peach pies or, worse yet, the frozen supermarket version. What if Jeanne had never recorded Aunt Naomi's Chocolate Fudge Cake (page 80)? It would be a sad and rainy day.

Make your own family cookbook and save a recipe.

Viola's Kentucky Peach Pie

*N*o pie could be easier or more delicious than this. Use only fresh, ripe peaches picked as close to home as possible. Best yet, pack a picnic and go to a pick-yourself orchard. Once you have picked enough peaches for several pies, spread a blanket on the ground and reward yourself for your hard work. Should a peach slice find its way into a glass of crisp white wine, you have worked hard indeed. If the pie won't get made otherwise, by all means, go ahead and use a good quality name-brand prepared pie crust.

1 cup sugar

1 stick (4 ounces) butter, at room
   temperature

⅓ cup flour

1 egg

1¼ teaspoons vanilla extract

4 to 5 large peaches, sliced (about
   5 cups)

1 recipe Marie Dugan's Pie Crust
   (page 83), or your favorite pie crust

Preheat oven to 350° F.

Using an electric mixer, combine sugar, butter, flour, egg, and vanilla, until well blended. Fold in peach slices and mix gently until peaches are well coated.

Line a 9-inch pie pan with 1 round of unbaked pie crust and pour in filling. Top with second round of pie crust and crimp edges. Prick a few holes for vents on top.

Bake pie for 1 hour. Let cool to room temperature before slicing.

MAKES 1 9-INCH PIE

Aunt Naomi's Chocolate Fudge Cake

*R*ecipe rescuer Jeanne Sach collected this cake recipe from the files of her aunt. Aunt Naomi and her husband, Joe, owned a shrimp business in South Carolina, but she still found time to volunteer in the church. This cake is made with ingredients you are likely to have on hand and, like loaves and fishes, seems to extend itself to serve an entire congregation. Should there be leftovers, this rich cake stays moist.

CAKE

2 cups instant flour

2 cups sugar

1 cup cold water

1 stick (4 ounces) butter

⅓ cup vegetable oil

4 teaspoons unsweetened cocoa powder

½ cup buttermilk

2 eggs, beaten

1 teaspoon baking soda

1 teaspoon cinnamon

FROSTING

1 stick (4 ounces) butter

¼ cup unsweetened cocoa powder

⅓ cup milk

1 teaspoon vanilla extract

1 1-pound box confectioners' sugar

Preheat oven to 350° F. Spray a 9-by-13-inch baking pan with nonstick spray.

Make the cake: Sift flour and sugar together. Set aside. In a medium saucepan, bring water, butter, oil, and cocoa powder to a boil. Add flour mixture and blend well. Add buttermilk, eggs, baking soda, and cinnamon and pour into the prepared pan. Bake for 25 to 30 minutes or until a toothpick inserted in the center comes out clean. Transfer to a rack to cool.

Make the frosting: Combine all the ingredients in a medium saucepan and bring just to a boil, stirring constantly until smooth. Do not boil. Pour over the cake while still warm. Let cool completely before cutting.

MAKES 16 2-BY-3-INCH SLICES

Kitchen Wisdom

Instant flour is a low-protein flour that is most commonly used in gravies and sauces because it dissolves easily. It is sold in thirteen-ounce canisters. For use in baking, cake flour is a reasonable substitute.

Marie Dugan's Pie Crust

My grandmother made remarkable pie crust, although she never handled it with the delicacy that so many experts demand. She was, however, able to measure flour in her hand by weight and would always caution me that the flour should feel slightly heavier on a rainy day versus a dry day. I suspect the keys to her success were the attention to the ratio of flour to shortening to liquid and the fact that she used lard, which is lower in moisture content than shortening or butter.

3 cups flour

2 teaspoons salt

1 teaspoon baking powder

1 cup shortening

6 to 8 tablespoons ice water

In a food processor or large bowl, mix dry ingredients together. Cut in shortening until mixture resembles coarse crumbs. Sprinkle cold water over the mixture 1 tablespoon at a time, tossing to blend. Add only enough water to form the dough into a cohesive ball. Put in plastic wrap and refrigerate for at least 20 minutes.

Divide dough in half and roll out each half into a round. Makes 2 single crust pies or 1 double crust. If you only need 1 single crust, freeze the second for future use.

MAKES 2 9-INCH CRUSTS

Marshmallows

*T*his recipe was one of my mother-in-law's contributions to a church cookbook. She also made her own marshmallow creme because she figured it only cost eleven cents to make at the time. While most of us today would think the cost of the labor outweighed any savings, this is a whole lot more fun than buying a bag of marshmallows. You'll be surprised at the taste, too. It's purer, with a lighter texture. Perfect for Hot Chocolate (page 177).

You can really make these any size, depending on use. For hot chocolate, I like big luxurious two-inch squares. For a more confection-like presentation, I like to cut them into one-and-a-half-inch rectangles and roll them in toasted coconut, nuts, or finely chopped chocolate or candy.

2 ¼-ounce envelopes gelatin (a scant
   2 tablespoons)

1½ cups water, divided

2 cups sugar

⅛ teaspoon salt

1 teaspoon vanilla extract

1 cup confectioners' sugar, for
   dusting

about 5 cups coconut or nuts, for
   rolling, optional

Spray an 8-inch square glass baking dish with nonstick cooking spray or butter liberally. Set aside.

In a large bowl of an electric mixer, soak gelatin in ¾ cup water for 5 minutes.

In a medium saucepan, boil sugar and remaining ¾ cup water until it spins a thread (235° F).

With the electric mixer on low speed, carefully pour sugar syrup over gelatin in a slow, steady stream and beat until mixture is light and frothy.

Add salt and vanilla. Beat for several minutes until the mixture is the consistency of a thick meringue.

Pour marshmallow into prepared pan and let stand for several hours to set up.

Cut marshmallow into squares with a knife dipped in warm water. Set on a tray lightly dusted with confectioners' sugar. If desired, roll in toasted or plain coconut, nuts, or finely chopped chocolate or candy.

MAKES 16 LARGE MARSHMALLOWS

Kitchen Wisdom

Marshmallows are a candy and will react badly to humidity. Try to store them somewhere other than the kitchen, which is a humid and unstable environment. I think the flavor develops as they set up so they are best eaten the next day.

For a festive look, tint plain coconut by adding a few drops of food coloring to half a teaspoon of water and tossing one cup coconut with it in a plastic bag until it is evenly colored.

MESSY FOOD

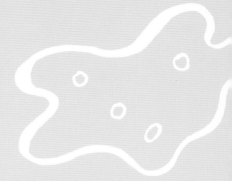

As a food stylist making beautiful food for the camera, I would spend hours gluing sesame seeds artfully on a bun and arranging rice on a plate one grain at a time. On one commercial shoot I spent ten hours locked in a small room looking at thousands of Kaiser rolls and presenting a dozen of the most flawless as "heroes" for the shot.

Food styling is all about perfection. Or more accurately, somebody else's idea of the perfect version of a dish. But frankly, I like my bagels burned. Maybe it's those overcooked vegetables of my childhood meals coming back to life, but I can't eat a bagel outside of the home because no one will char it to my desired degree of doneness. Give me carbon or just give me cornflakes!

As a caterer I developed a reputation for my carved vegetable crudité displays. At times no one would eat them because they were deemed "artistic." For a while I took this as a compliment. Looking back, I think it was silly to spend so much effort making a dish that no one would eat. Lately, food fashion seems to lean toward serving a plate of garnishes. It takes so long for the chef to arrange the plate your food is cold by the time it leaves the kitchen.

Tall food, nouvelle food, and sauce-painted plates may impress, but it's honest-to-goodness real food that we reach for in times of stress. Good old-fashioned comfort food. The stuff that sticks to your ribs, makes you slap your feet, and lick your fingers. It's what I call messy food. It's not arranged, no pretense. Just good food.

Garnish is not a word that goes with messy food. At the most, if it is a brown main-dish item, a little parsley to add color; a fruit slice if it is a dessert. Anything more than that is superfluous and anything resembling a drizzle around the rim of the plate is downright blasphemous.

Most often messy food is served family-style with big bowls passed around the table and a suitably large spoon for portioning a scoop. In certain situations, it is acceptable to by-pass the serving platter and bring the cooking vessel directly to the table. Generally speaking this is reserved for times of acute distress and immediate need for comfort. Or when someone forgot to run the dishwasher. Two conditions that may not be mutually exclusive, I might add.

Messy food can be eaten with your fingers: fried chicken, big overstuffed sandwiches, and sticky buns. There are different finger-eating styles. There's the "I'll just pick" in which food is pulled off in small bites so that the diner can delude herself into thinking she's eating less than she is. A more manly approach is the "gusto" style in which a certain degree of ripping lends a *Tom Jones* quality.

The use of anything more than a fork or fingers should make a comfort food suspect. Take brisket, for example. Properly cooked, a brisket is a slab of meat that has fallen apart—precluding the need for a knife. If you are going for comfort, you ought not to have to work so hard.

Desserts must be just a shade toward "too sweet." Otherwise, where's the comfort? Anything with whipped cream on it gets extra points.

There's a bumper sticker that says life is messy. It's true. And a regret is most often soothed by a dish that is sometimes imperfect. A dish so close to the bone, it is just what it is and there is no need to dress it up. These recipes are sure to comfort both big and small regrets.

Cement Cake

The unappetizing name belies the fact that this is a sublimely light meringue. When the cake comes out of the oven it falls, creating cracks and fissures that look like cement. My brother and I began calling it cement cake, much to our mother's chagrin, as it was one of her best offerings. The original recipe came from my grandmother's neighbor and was topped with "tinned peaches" but I prefer fresh fruit. I once thought it had its origins in a Pavlova (a creamy meringue that is piped onto a sheet pan), but discovered a similar recipe called Schaum Torte in *The Molly Goldberg Jewish Cookbook*.

CAKE

6 egg whites

2 cups sugar

2 teaspoons vanilla extract

2 teaspoons apple cider vinegar

TOPPING

2 cups heavy cream

1 pint fresh strawberries, hulled and halved (reserve some whole berries for garnish)

Preheat oven to 300° F.

Make the cake: Using an electric mixer, beat egg whites until stiff. Add sugar slowly while beating at a low speed. Blend in vanilla and vinegar. Spoon batter into a 9-inch springform pan. Bake for 45 minutes. Remove cake from oven and let cool.

Make the topping: Just before serving, whip cream. Arrange berries on top of cake. Spread the cream on the top and sides of the cake. If desired, garnish with reserved berries.

MAKES 8 SLICES

Sticky Buns

In Pennsylvania, you'll find these extra-rich cinnamon buns at all the Amish stands. I use the same dough and make one pan of sticky buns while another pan of Parker House Rolls (page 27) is rising in the refrigerator. The Parker House rolls freeze well, but the sticky buns you just have to eat all at once!

1 recipe Easy Yeast Dough (page 73)	⅓ cup light corn syrup
1 stick (4 ounces) butter, plus	¾ cup toasted pecan halves
1 tablespoon butter, melted	1 tablespoon cinnamon
1 cup dark brown sugar	1 cup raisins

Preheat oven to 375° F.

Divide dough in half. Reserve 1 portion for a second pan of buns or another use. Spray a 9-by-9-by-3-inch baking pan (see Kitchen Wisdom on the next page) with nonstick cooking spray. Set aside.

In a large saucepan, bring 1 stick butter, brown sugar, and corn syrup to a boil. Cook over medium heat for about 1 minute, or until butter is melted and sugar is dissolved to form a syrup. Pour into prepared pan and spread pecans evenly over the bottom. Set aside.

Roll dough half into 14-by-9-inch rectangle. Brush melted butter over the top. Sprinkle cinnamon and then raisins evenly over the top and press slightly into dough.

Roll up dough from the long side into a 14-inch log. Pinch ends and seam closed. Cut into 9 1½-inch slices and place cut side down on pecans in pan.

Bake buns for 25 to 30 minutes or until brown. Let cool for 15 minutes and invert on a serving platter.

MAKES 9 BUNS

Kitchen Wisdom

Nine-inch-square pans that are three inches in depth are hard to come by, so these can be made in the standard two-inch pan with one adaptation. The "goop" will boil over so put a large rimmed baking sheet on the rack under the pan to catch the spill—a technique that saves oven cleanup no matter what size pan you use.

Noodle Kugel

I had never had kugel until it appeared on the potluck table at my son's elementary school. Of course, I made it a point to become friends with the person attached to the dish. There are about as many versions of kugel as there are Jewish grandmothers. It seems to me that they are all good, but everyone prefers the one that they grew up with. I like Janet Lipes's kugel recipe the best probably because it's the one that my son had at all those school potlucks. Although it tastes sweet, kugel is most often served as a side dish. It's like having a little dessert with the main course.

TOPPING

½ cup cornflake crumbs

⅓ cup sugar

1 teaspoon cinnamon

KUGEL

5 ounces fine egg noodles, cooked
   and drained (2 cups cooked)

3 eggs

8 ounces cottage cheese

8 ounces sour cream

½ cup sugar

4 tablespoons butter, melted

1 teaspoon vanilla extract

Preheat oven to 350° F.

Make the topping: In a bowl, mix cornflake crumbs, sugar, and cinnamon. Set aside.

Make kugel: Grease an 8-inch-square baking pan and place noodles in the pan.

In a blender, purée eggs, cottage cheese, sour cream, sugar, butter, and vanilla. Pour over noodles and sprinkle topping over all.

Bake kugel for 1 hour or until pudding is cooked through and slightly puffy.

MAKES 16 2-INCH SQUARES

Kitchen Wisdom

Janet says kugel may be made a day ahead and refrigerated. That may work in her house, but in mine someone always finds it.

Banana Pudding

This is not at all like the banana pudding recipes on the back of the cookie box. The "pudding" is more like an old-fashioned boiled custard. My tasters all clamored for more, exclaiming "it's a soufflé, it's pudding—no, it's better than both." At first glance you'll think this makes too much, but there is never enough for all the friends and family who will hound you for seconds. Recipe rescuer Shelly Summers taught me how to make this exquisite dish.

SAUCE

1 12-ounce can evaporated milk

2¼ cups whole milk

1¼ cups sugar

1 stick (4 ounces) butter

3 egg yolks, beaten until creamy

1 tablespoon cinnamon

1 teaspoon nutmeg

⅛ teaspoon salt

PUDDING

2 12-ounce boxes vanilla wafers

7 to 10 peeled bananas, depending on size, sliced into ¼-inch rounds

Make the sauce: Combine evaporated milk, whole milk, sugar, butter, egg yolks, cinnamon, nutmeg, and salt in a medium saucepan. Bring to a boil, stirring constantly. Reduce the heat and simmer for at least 20 minutes. Keep an eye on the pudding, since it boils over easily.

Layer the pudding: Line the bottom of a 2½-quart casserole with the cookies by overlapping them slightly in a shingle pattern. Top with a flat layer of banana slices. Shingle another layer of cookies, then banana, then cookies, leaving enough cookies and bananas for 1 more layer.

When the sauce is slightly thickened—it will be like thick sludge—ladle it ½ cup at a time over the pudding layers while it is still warm, letting it absorb between additions, until you have used about 3 cups. Keep the sauce warm while you are working.

Place the final layers of bananas and cookies on the pudding and slowly pour additional sauce over the top. If necessary, use a fork to push the edges aside to allow as much sauce as possible to seep into the cookies. There may be sauce leftover.

Refrigerate for several hours to firm up.

MAKES ABOUT 16 SERVINGS

Kitchen Wisdom

Shelly notes that there may be more sauce than needed, "so just get over it." You can pass around a pitcher of sauce to spoon over the pudding, if desired. Extra sauce is also delicious over ice cream, or let any little helping hands just grab a spoonful or two, just like my grandmother used to give me little crescents of extra pie crust sprinkled with cinnamon sugar. I almost liked it better than the pie because it was a little extra something my grandmother made just for me.

Recipe Rescuer Shelly Summers

Shelly Summers can make you feel like the most important person in the world. When she says your name the word slides off her tongue like a sweet syrup spun around a favorite spoon. In her kitchen, comfort is served up in the food and the conversation.

Shelly grew up in Mississippi and knows her way around a kitchen. She has developed that keen sixth sense of a true cook and watching her is more instructive than any TV show. No need to measure or check temperatures. The most elaborate tool I've seen her use is a dinner fork. She is a walking cookbook.

Shelly's cooking is an extension of her. She enjoys nurturing people and has great respect and understanding for everyone. When we cook together we swap recipes as well as stories about our lives. While chicken quietly bubbles in the pan, she tells me the story of her mother, who was a cook in a "whites only" restaurant during the 1950s.

"Mama made $17 a week, which was more than the white girls but, oh my, she could cook," recalls Shelly. "One time she saw a fight between two white men. They tried to get her to talk. She didn't want to. She just wanted to mind her own business."

"Well," says Shelly, "this white man hit her—slapped her hard trying to get her to talk. It was the time a black person went to jail if they hit a white person, but my mama grabbed a leg of lamb and she started pounding that man." Shelly shakes her head.

"When the police came," she continues, "the owner of the restaurant took care of things. He just said, knowing how much everyone liked her cooking, you know, if Anna Mae goes to jail there won't be food tomorrow."

Shelly laughs. "Well, that was that! My mama stayed out of jail. Oh, my mama could cook." Shelly's mama could cook and she certainly passed it down to her daughter, too.

Shelly's Fried Chicken

I ate this chicken for a year and pronounced it the best I had ever eaten. Imagine my surprise to discover that the secret ingredient was Kool-Aid. Granted, it's just a little bit to "boost the flavor," but because I tend not to like too many processed ingredients and can be a bit pedantic about it, I had to laugh at myself.

SEASONING MIX

1 envelope (1 teaspoon) Sazón
 Spanish-style coriander and
 annatto seasoning blend (see
 Kitchen Wisdom on the next page)

1 teaspoon Accent (MSG), optional,
 or ½ teaspoon garlic salt

½ teaspoon lemonade Kool-Aid
 powder

½ teaspoon black pepper

CHICKEN

3 to 4 pounds chicken parts

1 teaspoon salt

1 teaspoon black pepper

oil, for frying, preferably canola

1½ cups flour

Blend together Sazón, Accent, Kool-Aid, and pepper. Set the seasoning mix aside.

In a large bowl, wash chicken in several changes of salted water. Remove visible fat. Drain, leaving a little water clinging to the chicken. Sprinkle salt and pepper over the skin, rubbing the seasonings into the meat. Set aside.

Add oil to come 1 inch up the sides of a deep fryer or large heavy pan. Heat to 375° F (follow manufacturer's directions for your appliance or see page 185 for deep-frying instructions).

While the oil is heating, sprinkle 1 teaspoon of the prepared seasoning mix over the chicken. Blend remaining seasoning mix with flour in a large bag. Shake chicken pieces, 1 at a time, in the bag to thoroughly coat.

When the oil is heated, carefully add as many chicken pieces, 1 piece at a time, as will comfortably fit in the pan. Cover the pan and steam the meat for 5 minutes. Uncover and cook 20 to 25 minutes more, turning several times. Chicken is done when a thermometer inserted into the meat registers 180° F, or the juices run clear.

SERVES 4

Kitchen Wisdom

Shelly has no need for thermometers or gadgets. She has fine-tuned her senses to know when the oil is hot enough by tossing a pinch of flour in the oil and watching how fast it bubbles. She knows the chicken is done to perfection by keeping a fork hot in the oil. When the hot fork is inserted in the meat and removed, Shelly knows the chicken is cooked if there is resistance to the fork. It takes years to develop that level of skill and it is magnificent to observe.

— ·· —

Sazón is a blend of coriander, annatto, and other seasonings. It is widely available in the Spanish section of the grocery store. If you cannot find it or choose not to use it, substitute equal amounts of paprika and garlic salt.

Macaroni and Cheese

The beauty of mac' and cheese is that each generation can add its own special touch—making the bread crumbs from scratch or refining the choice of cheese. This is my grandmother's method for preparing macaroni and cheese. It is basic and simple (the canned milk substitutes for a white sauce) and beats anything out of a box or supermarket freezer.

1 pound elbow macaroni

2 12-ounce cans evaporated milk

½ pound New York State white
    cheddar, grated

½ pound New York State yellow
    cheddar, grated

½ teaspoon salt

¼ teaspoon black pepper

⅔ cup fresh white bread crumbs

⅓ cup aged Asiago cheese, grated
    (more, if desired)

Preheat oven to 350° F. Spray a 9-by-17-inch pan with nonstick cooking spray.

Cook macaroni according to package directions until just barely cooked, about 7 minutes. Rinse and drain and spread evenly in the prepared pan. Set aside.

In a medium saucepan, heat evaporated milk almost to a boil. Remove from heat and add the yellow and white cheeses, stirring until melted. Add salt and pepper.

Pour cheese sauce over the macaroni and mix well. Mix the bread crumbs and Asiago together and spread over the top of the casserole. If desired, top with more Asiago. Bake the casserole for 25 to 30 minutes,

or until the top is brown and the cheese bubbles. Let set for 5 minutes before serving.

SERVES 8 FOR A MAIN DISH, MORE FOR A SIDE DISH

Kitchen Wisdom

If you like your macaroni and cheese creamy, undercook it slightly. If you like it brown and crusty, add a little extra cooking time or stick it under the broiler. And no one ever said a little extra cheese wouldn't be a nice addition.

Lentils and Rice (Riz-be-Adees)

This dish defines comfort food for Georgette Macbeth. She recalls her mother, Helen Hamaty, making unbelievable meals every night in the tradition of her Lebanese heritage for a family of five children. While Helen suggests serving this with chicken, Georgette recalls Riz-be-Adees as part of a meatless Lenten menu. Its charm is also in the simplicity of preparation.

4 cups water

1 teaspoon salt

1 cup lentils, rinsed and drained

1 cup long-grain rice

1 large onion, diced (about 2 cups)

½ cup olive oil

In a medium saucepan, bring water and salt to a boil over high heat. Add lentils, cover, and simmer for 20 minutes or until lentils are almost tender.

Add rice, cover, and cook 20 minutes more. Remove from heat and keep covered, allowing rice to steam.

Meanwhile, in a medium sauté pan, heat olive oil and add onion. Cook until onion is golden brown. Pour over rice and lentils and serve.

MAKES ABOUT 6 CUPS

Barbecue Ham Sandwich

I've been eating this sandwich so long I don't know where it came from. Despite the long cook time, it requires hardly any attention and leftovers can be frozen for another day. Serve on buns or bread (preferably a softer type to hold the sauce—sometimes referred to as "soppin'" bread) and with Freezer Pickles (page 61).

1 2- to 3-pound smoked boneless
   pork shoulder

1 tablespoon Dijon mustard

1 tablespoon maple syrup

3 cups Barbecue Sauce (page 105) or
   use bottled

buns or white bread

Preheat oven to 350° F.

Slice ham in half lengthwise and place cut side down in a greased small, shallow roasting pan.

Blend mustard and maple syrup together and brush over the top of the ham. Cover and bake for 1½ hours. Uncover and bake another hour, or until browned and falling apart. During the cooking time check occasionally and add a little water to the pan to keep residue in the pan from burning.

Let cool enough to handle, then chop into small pieces. Mix with barbecue sauce.

MAKES ABOUT 6 TO 8 SANDWICHES

Barbecue Sauce

*M*any years ago I went to a party that almost turned into a Hatfield and McCoys brawl. The dispute was over the host's secret barbecue sauce ingredient and his absolute refusal to share the recipe. Frankly, the intrigue probably added more to the sauce than the ingredient. Rather than enter the fray, I set out to create my own sauce which I gladly share. Feel free to add your own secret ingredient! I like to add some dried chiles such as chipotle along with the other seasonings.

1 medium onion, finely chopped (about ⅔ cup)

1 tablespoon olive oil

3 cups puréed or strained tomatoes (about 26 ounces)

½ cup cider vinegar

½ cup brown sugar

2 tablespoons sweet Hungarian paprika

1 tablespoon molasses

1 tablespoon Worcestershire sauce

1 tablespoon dry mustard

1 teaspoon celery seeds

In a medium saucepan, sauté onion in oil until translucent. Add remaining ingredients and simmer over medium heat for 30 minutes, stirring occasionally and scraping down the sides. (May be frozen for future use.)

MAKES ABOUT 3 CUPS

Mustard Sauce

_H_ere's a recipe that demonstrates how the lack of certain ingredients can sometimes make a recipe endangered. When Nancy Ennis passed this recipe on to me she told me about her aunt, Genevive Stewart Witherspoon, who lived in Kemmerer, Wyoming. She loved to cook and collected many recipes such as this one. Unfortunately, she couldn't buy the dry mustard in Wyoming, so Nancy recalls her mother sending Genevive a steady supply from the East Coast. Fortunately, dry mustard is readily available today.

This is similar to a boiled dressing that was popular in the forties and fifties, but has a little more zing. Spread this on sandwiches or use as a dipping sauce for chunks of cheese or hot appetizers such as spinach balls.

¼ **cup dry mustard such as Colman's**	**2 eggs**
¼ **cup sugar**	**1 cup canned evaporated milk**
1 tablespoon plus 2 teaspoons flour	½ **cup herbed vinegar**
¼ **teaspoon salt**	**2 tablespoons butter**
¼ **teaspoon black pepper**	

In a double boiler, sift mustard, sugar, flour, salt, and pepper together. Add eggs and milk and beat well. Cook over simmering water, whisking constantly, until mixture thickens. Add vinegar and butter and blend well. Remove from heat and let cool. Sauce will thicken as it cools. Pour into a clean container and refrigerate for up to 1 week.

MAKES ABOUT 1 ½ CUPS

Welsh Rarebit

*T*oo many mediocre versions of Welsh rarebit gave this dish a bad name. The British originally served this at high tea, making it much more elegant than our cafeteria "something on a shingle" image. Unlike the rarebits that use a white sauce or other thickener, this recipe is all cheese and full of flavor. The final broil makes a nice top crust, while underneath the cheese is a velvety sauce. Welsh rarebit is traditionally served with tomatoes, but I like to serve it with Tomato Soup (page 148) for an upper-crust grilled cheese and soup repast. There's not much else going on in this dish, so superior English beer and cheddar is essential.

¼ cup English beer or ale

1 teaspoon dry mustard

⅛ teaspoon cayenne pepper

⅛ teaspoon Worcestershire sauce

1 pound English Farmhouse cheddar, finely diced (about 2 cups)

6 slices white bread, such as Pullman or sandwich loaf, crusts removed, cut in half on the diagonal and toasted

In a double boiler, mix beer, mustard, cayenne, and Worcestershire sauce. Add cheese by handfuls, stirring constantly to make a smooth sauce.

In a 9-inch pie plate, layer toast triangles. Pour sauce over bread and broil until cheese is bubbly, 2 to 3 minutes.

SERVES 4

Thelma's Brisket

I remember this dish appearing at just about every large family get-together. Fortunately, someone thought to put the recipe down on paper. Brisket is a definite "make and take" dish because it can be reheated and leftovers make great sandwiches. A colleague mentioned that brisket often appears in his neighborhood as part of the "brisket brigade." That is, a suitable time after a man has become a widower, a stream of widows will make their way to the door, brisket in hand.

BRISKET

4 to 5 pound brisket, trimmed of all fat

1 tablespoon sweet Hungarian
   paprika

1 teaspoon freshly ground black
   pepper

½ teaspoon salt

3 onions, thinly sliced (about 2½ cups)

GRAVY

1 large potato

1 pound white mushrooms, quartered

Preheat oven to 300° F.

Line a 13-by-9-inch baking pan with 1 sheet of heavy-duty aluminum foil large enough to make a tight packet around the brisket.

Prepare the brisket: Place the brisket on the foil, trimmed side up. Season with paprika, pepper, and salt. Place onions on top and make your packet. Make a tight seal to keep all the juices in for later use.

Roast in the oven for about 5 hours. Remove from the oven and let rest for 10 to 15 minutes. Open the foil carefully. Remove meat and pour juices into a saucepan.

Make the gravy: Peel and finely grate the raw potato. Add potato and mushrooms to brisket juices. Simmer until potato is cooked and gravy is slightly thickened. Serve with sliced brisket.

SERVES 8 TO 10

Kitchen Wisdom

A brisket is an easy way to entertain and is especially good for a buffet table. This recipe can be made ahead, sliced, and frozen. Reheat, covered, in the oven or microwave oven.

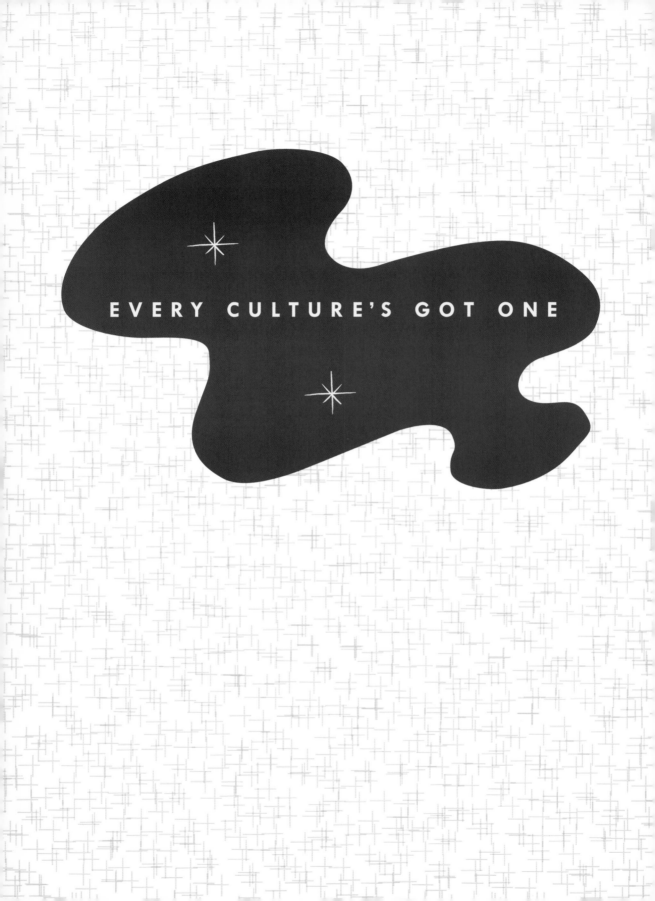

EVERY CULTURE'S GOT ONE

*I*t's a magical street, South Ninth Street in Philadelphia. At times it feels Brigadoon-like, transporting you to a different place in time. You can almost see the past: vendors hawking food and wares from horse-drawn carts; the movie character, Rocky, jogging up a street lined with burning trash barrels; and— always—children, minded by a neighborhood of adults, running in and out of the stores looking for excitement.

The Italian Market, as the six blocks running between Federal and Christian are known, is the oldest and largest working outdoor market in the United States. At any given time—the count varies—there are roughly forty produce stores; seven meat markets, including a sausage maker; four stores that sell imported cheeses; four fish markets; two pasta stores; two bread bakeries; a coffee stand; a gourmet take-out; and a kitchenware retailer. On the outskirts are several Asian grocery stores.

I can't imagine there is anywhere else quite like it. Old oil barrels still line the streets and the street vendors burn the produce boxes to brave the predawn cold for setup. The sight of purveyors warming their hands on a cold day is such a landmark that everyone accepts the open flame in a public space. Tin awnings provide shelter for salesmen and customers alike. Shoppers jostle for attention and first-timers learn quickly not to handle the produce or they will be reprimanded like a kid caught without his homework.

It's a place where people still live and work for a piece of the American Dream. The market may carry the name "Italian" but it is a microcosm of the immigrant experience. In the early 20th century, newly arrived immigrants to Ninth Street began selling items in front of their houses. Eventually stores took over the ground floor and living quarters moved upstairs. It's the classic formula: an immigrant community introduces products they are familiar with, and when demand is eventually developed, it helps to grow a business community and leads to economic success.

The first group to make a presence on Ninth Street was primarily Jewish. The next wave was Italian, and that influence still exists today. Although the apartments over the stores are gone and many retailers commute from the suburbs, there remains a strong familial link between store owners that is part of the fabric of the community. Today the ethnic enclaves that exist on the fringe of the market include Vietnamese, Cambodian, Korean, and most recently, Mexicans who have come to work in the city's restaurants.

Food has always drawn people to the market. It is entertainment shopping. You can watch pasta being rolled out in Talluto's window, and taste an authentic scrambled egg and Pennsylvania scrapple (think polenta and boiled pig parts) sandwich at George's Sandwich Shop. Sonny D' Angelo prepares a veritable Noah's Ark of game meats, and the basement bakery of Isgro's perfumes the air with the smell of fresh cannoli shells.

On other side of the street you can get Vietnamese hoagies—an Asian take on a Philadelphia tradition. In the vast Asian grocery store, I'm almost always approached by someone offering to help me identify the produce, or keep me from making a major mistake at the rows and rows of large live fish tanks. These are not store clerks; they are customers only too happy to share their culture.

When you see a variety of global foods within blocks of each other, you begin to notice similarities. The technique of taking a rice pancake and filling it with a Vietnamese vegetable stuffing really isn't all that different from a tortilla stuffed with refried beans and rolled into a burrito. Italian meatballs and spaghetti is essentially ground meat surrounded by a noodle; ditto for a steamed Chinese pork dumpling. How all these likenesses came about makes a career for food historians and fun speculation for the rest of us. The fact remains a place like the Italian Market plays an important role in ensuring that these unique ethnic ingredients, techniques, and dishes do not disappear—do not become victims of assimilation.

Try these dishes. You may be surprised to find how close to home they are to your family recipes.

Koenigsberger Klopse

I was discussing meatballs one day with Maiken Scott, the producer of the radio show *A Chef's Table*. She recalled that in her childhood she hated a meatball dish her mother served. I asked her what the ingredients were and, as she told me, we both piped up at the same time, "actually that sounds pretty good." We got the recipe and when Maiken tried these meatballs as an adult she really liked them. Sometimes it's not just the treasured recipes of our childhood, but also the reviled ones that need to be resurrected. It's worth revisiting those cast-off recipes. Serve these meatballs with boiled potatoes and a salad.

MEATBALLS
1 day-old hard roll
4 anchovy fillets, cut into small pieces
1 egg
½ pound ground beef
½ pound ground veal or pork
2 tablespoons grated onion
several grindings of freshly ground
   black pepper

SAUCE
3 tablespoons butter
3 tablespoons flour
2 cups milk
1 cup chicken broth
2 tablespoons capers

Make the meatballs: Soak roll in water to cover until soft. Squeeze dry and set aside ½ cup.

Mash anchovies against the side of a medium bowl. Add egg and beat well. Mix in bread. Stir in meat, onion, and pepper. Refrigerate until thoroughly chilled. Form into 16 balls (a scant quarter cup each). Set aside.

Make the sauce: Melt butter in a large sauté pan. Stir in flour and cook, stirring constantly, until butter bubbles and flour is cooked. Whisk in milk and chicken broth until smooth.

Bring sauce to a boil and add meatballs and capers. Reduce heat and simmer, uncovered for 25 to 30 minutes or until the meatballs are cooked through. Turn the meatballs several times during cooking.

MAKES ABOUT 16 MEATBALLS, OR SERVES 4

Kibbeh

I wanted to learn how to make kibbeh, a Middle Eastern dish with ground meat mixed with bulgur wheat, but I was having trouble finding someone who made it. When I finally met Jackie Decker, she was reluctant to make kibbeh without the guiding hand of her mother's experience. We came up with the recipe rescuer idea to "teleconference." Her mom was on stand-by, answering our questions as we made the dish. Happily, we did just fine. Kibbeh can also be made in layers in a large pan; however, I prefer the meatballs because the stuffing stays in place and makes it much easier to eat. It is also served raw, an uncommon practice in this country today.

MEATBALLS

¾ cup medium grade bulgur (see Kitchen Wisdom on the next page)

1 pound ground lamb

1 small onion, grated (about 3 to 4 tablespoons)

¾ teaspoon allspice

¾ teaspoon dried mint

½ teaspoon ground cumin

½ teaspoon salt

¼ teaspoon pepper

2 tablespoons olive oil

FILLING

⅓ pound lamb

1 tablespoon olive oil

¼ teaspoon ground allspice

¼ teaspoon dried mint

1 tablespoon finely chopped onion

2 tablespoons pine nuts, toasted

pita bread and yogurt, for serving

Make the meatball mixture: Rinse bulgur several times in cold water and place in a medium bowl. Cover with cold water and soak until softened, about 30 minutes.

In a large bowl, mix together ground lamb, onion, allspice, mint, cumin, salt, and pepper. Add ice to a bowl of water and set aside to dip your hands in while working. Drain bulgur and squeeze dry. Add to meat mixture by handfuls, kneading thoroughly after each addition to make a fine paste. Keep your hands clean by dipping into the ice water.

When the bulgur is incorporated and the mixture is like a paste, refrigerate until chilled, about 30 minutes.

Make the filling: Mince the lamb. In a medium saucepan, heat 1 tablespoon olive oil. Add meat and cook until browned. Add allspice, mint, and onion and cook for several minutes until the onion is translucent and the meat is thoroughly cooked. Add pine nuts. Set aside.

Form the meatballs: Make approximately 12 football-shaped balls (about ¼ cup each) with the meatball mixture. Using your thumb, make an indent in the center and place a scant tablespoon of the filling in the hole. Seal and press back into shape.

Heat remaining 2 tablespoons oil in a large sauté pan and add the meatballs in batches. Cook several minutes on all sides, until the meatballs are well-browned and cooked through. Drain and serve warm with pita bread and yogurt on the side.

MAKES ABOUT 12 MEATBALLS, OR SERVES 4

Kitchen Wisdom

Bulgur comes in coarse, medium, and fine grains. Bulgur—whole wheat kernels that have been par-boiled, dried, and ground—is not to be confused with cracked wheat.

Neapolitan Stuffed Peppers

*E*very culture may have a stuffed pepper, but in Italy it appears that every region's got their own. The following Neapolitan recipe has no meat or cheese and it is filled with pasta, making it a nice summer dish. Serve it warm or room temperature with a wedge of Italian sheep's milk cheese—a Pecorino Toscano table cheese with a glass of good Chianti is recommended. In that case, all movie jokes aside, some fresh fava beans would be the ideal accompaniment.

6 yellow or red bell peppers (about 2 pounds)

6 tablespoons olive oil

2 cloves garlic

1 cup canned chopped tomatoes (or about 2 fresh tomatoes, peeled and seeded)

½ cup good black Italian olives or kalamatas, pitted and chopped

3 to 4 anchovy fillets, mashed

2 tablespoons capers

1 tablespoon fresh oregano, chopped, plus oregano sprigs, for garnish

½ pound ditalini pasta, cooked according to package directions

Preheat oven to 375° F. Slice the tops off the peppers and reserve. Remove seeds and membrane. Set aside.

Heat 2 tablespoons olive oil in a medium skillet. Sauté garlic until just golden. Add tomatoes and simmer for about 5 minutes. Stir in olives, anchovies, capers, and oregano and mix well. Add pasta and toss well.

Stuff peppers with pasta mixture and arrange upright in a shallow baking pan. Put tops back on peppers. Drizzle the remaining ¼ cup olive oil over the tops. Bake for 50 to 55 minutes, or until peppers still hold their shape but are slightly shriveled.

Serve warm or at room temperature, garnished with a fresh oregano sprig.

SERVES 6

Italian Wedding Soup

I lived in a small New Jersey town along the Delaware River before it became gentrified. It was the custom for several of the matrons on the block to bring folding lawn chairs out on the sidewalk after dinner. The events of the day and state of the world were discussed with enthusiasm. One day, the ladies were quite horrified to discover I had come out before the dinner dishes had been washed and even more distressed to learn I was leaving them for my husband to do. I was the topic of conversation that night!

My neighbor made the most wonderful tiny veal meatballs, but I could never get the recipe from her. This recipe is a close second, however. She also put these meatballs in lasagna, which made my husband exclaim he would do the dishes for a month if I did that too. There are many versions of this soup and probably just as many stories about the name. While you would need a food historian to unravel the myth and lore, I don't believe the soup's name derived from being served at weddings. The marriage refers to the ideal combination of the ingredients.

MEATBALLS

½ pound ground veal

⅓ cup dry bread crumbs

1 egg, beaten

2 teaspoons grated onion

¼ teaspoon salt

⅛ teaspoon black pepper

⅛ teaspoon nutmeg

SOUP

6 cups chicken stock

5 to 6 cups chopped escarole (about ½ head) (see Kitchen Wisdom on page 120)

½ cup acine di pepe pasta or orzo

½ cup grated Romano cheese

Make the meatballs: Mix veal, bread crumbs, egg, onion, salt, pepper, and nutmeg well. Form into very tiny, compact meatballs about ½ teaspoon each. There will be about 65 meatballs. Set aside.

Make the soup: Bring chicken stock to a boil, reduce heat and add escarole, pasta, and meatballs. Simmer for 20 minutes or until the meatballs and escarole are cooked through.

Serve steamy hot and pass with cheese.

MAKES ABOUT 8 CUPS

Kitchen Wisdom

Escarole and chicory are often confused and to make things even more confusing, chicory is sometimes confused with curly endive. Escarole has a sweeter flavor, and much broader leaves. Curly endive is, obviously, curly and has thinner leaves. You'll often see it used as a throw-away garnish in restaurants which is a shame because it is tasty. Both are used primarily in salads, but don't overlook the cooked possibilities of these greens.

Stuffed Peppers

I learned how to make this dish from an Italian-American in Brooklyn. This stuffing is like an individual meatloaf wrapped in a vegetable. In fact, when I make meatloaf this is basically how I do it. You'll want plenty of leftovers because just like meatloaf, this dish is even better the next day.

You say tomato, I say marinara. Personally, I prefer the lighter taste of marinara sauce. The resulting dish will have a slightly thinner sauce than one made with tomato sauce. Either way, the sauce will be thicker or thinner depending on how juicy the peppers are.

1 day-old hard roll or white bread

6 green bell peppers (about 2 pounds)

1 egg, beaten

¼ cup milk

½ cup diced onion

½ cup freshly grated Parmigiano-Reggiano cheese

½ teaspoon dried oregano

¼ teaspoon black pepper

1 pound lean ground beef

3 cups tomato sauce or marinara

Preheat oven to 400° F.

Soak roll or bread in water until soft. Squeeze dry and set aside ½ cup.

Wash and dry peppers. Slice off the top (about ¼ to ½ inch). Remove stem, ribs, and seeds. Spray a 9-by-13-inch baking pan with nonstick cooking spray and place peppers upright in the pan. Set aside.

In a large bowl, mix egg and milk together. Blend in soaked bread, onion, cheese, oregano, and pepper. Add ground beef and knead until thoroughly mixed. Stuff peppers (about ½ cup each). Pour tomato sauce on top and bake for about 1 hour and 15 minutes or until sauce is bubbly and meat juices run clear.

SERVES 6

Kitchen Wisdom

My good colleague and radio host of *You Bet Your Garden,* Mike McGrath, recently solved a query I have been puzzling over for a long time. Bell peppers come in varying shapes and sizes. In particular, on the bottom they have two, three, or four "humps." Or, more correctly, "lobes" advises Mike. The two humpers are great for slicing into strips and, he explains, they also tend to be the thinnest-walled sweet peppers; three humps are best for slicing into rings because of their thicker walls; and the four humps are best for stuffing because the four lobes are stable standing on end. Mike says these are different types, and therefore, varieties of bell peppers. So what do you ask for to get the "hump of your choice" when you go to the store? Mike says to simply "use your eyes, dear, trying to learn the names will drive you crazy." He adds that if you wish to grow a certain variety, just look carefully at the pictures in seed catalogues, and remember that "Italian" usually means two, and "blocky" means three or four.

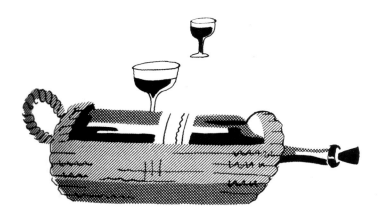

Recipe Rescuer Loretta Barrett Oden

Loretta first came to my attention when I was interviewing Shannon Scott of Native Seeds/SEARCH for the radio show *A Chef's Table*. Native Seeds/SEARCH is an organization dedicated to preserving traditional crop varieties of the American Southwest and northwest Mexico. They find, collect, grow, and redistribute heirloom seeds that would otherwise be lost to us.

It is one thing to save the seeds and grow the crops, but if no one knows how to cook these foods their rescue will be short-lived. That's how Loretta's name came up. Loretta grew up on the Citizen Potawatomi Indian Reservation in Oklahoma. As an adult, she was struck by the differences of the foods and customs between the Native American tribes across the country. This discovery led her to also explore the indigenous people of South America. As she began to understand the commonality between the various ingredients they used in their recipes, she created New World cuisine with Old World influences.

Loretta's dishes are as simple as grilled ear of sweet corn with chipotle oil or as complex as cedar planked salmon with wild huckleberry sauce, braised spinach, and quinoa pilaf. She'll cook with goat cheese, hearts of palm, and baby greens—all ingredients you'll find in the slick food magazines today. But she also uses ancient grains such as quinoa and wild rice, and meat can be as varied as venison, quail, rabbit, and bison.

Loretta believes food can be transforming. She sees food as a way to educate people about Native American culture and way of life. She's a believer in restorative methods of farming and notes, "We've gone beyond the notion of sustainable farming. We now have to heal the damage we've done."

Few chefs would know that red, blue, and yellow Indian corn require less water and fertilizer than standard hybrid corn. Nor would they care about the heritage of the foods they cook. Loretta, however, sees the dining table as no less than a bridge between cultures and the millennia. Her insight into our culinary heritage and her recipes can be found in her forthcoming PBS television series and companion book, *Seasoned with Spirit: A Native Cook's Journey*.

Ancho Chile Corn Fritters
with Pueblo Salsa

*I*n my opinion a fritter is a fried pancake, but at the very least they are culinary cousins. Loretta's use of native ingredients in a typical recipe such as a fritter is a hallmark of her recipe rescuing technique. Ancho chiles are a dried poblano chile indispensable to southwestern cooking. Loretta uses whole ancho chiles, but for simplicity I substitute ancho chile powder, which is available in most Mexican markets. A tomatillo is also known as a Mexican green tomato. While it won't be quite the same, you could substitute green tomatoes or canned tomatillo. Loretta fire-roasts her corn for added depth of flavor. She recommends serving these as an appetizer, but I also like them with a salad for lunch.

SALSA

3 tomatillos, chopped

1 large yellow tomato, chopped

⅓ cup red onion, chopped

2 jalapeño chiles, roasted, seeded, and minced

juice and zest of ½ lime

2 tablespoons chopped cilantro, plus cilantro sprigs for garnish

1 teaspoon chopped garlic

FRITTERS

½ cup flour

½ teaspoon ancho chile powder, or to taste

¼ teaspoon baking powder

⅛ teaspoon salt

1½ cup corn kernels

1 Granny Smith apple, peeled, cored, and julienned into 1-inch matchsticks

2 eggs, separated

corn oil, for frying

Make the salsa: In a medium nonreactive bowl, combine the tomatillos, tomato, red onion, jalapeño, lime juice and zest, cilantro, and garlic. Cover and refrigerate until ready to use.

Make the fritters: Mix together the flour, ancho chile powder, baking powder, and salt. Add the corn, apple, and egg yolks. Mix well and set aside.

In a large bowl, beat egg whites until soft peaks form. Fold into the chile mixture and let stand 10 minutes.

In a large, heavy pan, heat one inch of oil until it reaches 375° F. Spoon a heaping tablespoon of the corn mixture into the hot oil and flatten it slightly in the pan. Cook until golden brown on one side, about 2 minutes, turn and cook about 1 minute more. Drain on paper towels and keep in a warm oven until ready to serve.

Spoon salsa on top of each fritter and garnish with a cilantro sprig.

MAKES ABOUT 1 1/2 DOZEN

Kitchen Wisdom

To roast corn, pull the husks back without detaching them. Remove the silk and soak the corn and husks in water for at least ten minutes. Grill over hot coals, basting with corn oil and turning frequently for about three to five minutes.

Potato Pancakes

*M*ost often identified with Hanukkah, potato pancakes are delicious at other times of the year too. If you are only going to have them once a year, then by all means cook them in duck fat. The flavor is unbelievable. These are best served directly from the griddle, so some poor soul will be at the stove while others are eating. But it's not such a bad job—I love the little crispies that are left in the pan at the end.

1 tablespoon flour

1½ teaspoons salt

½ teaspoon baking powder

1½ pounds potatoes (2 cups), peeled grated, and squeezed dry

2 eggs, well beaten

2 tablespoon grated onion

1 to 2 tablespoons oil, for cooking

In a small bowl, blend together flour, salt, and baking powder. Mix potatoes, eggs, and onion together in a separate bowl. Sprinkle the flour mixture evenly over the potatoes and mix well.

Heat a large skillet over high heat and add the oil. Drop potato mixture by ⅓ cupfuls for large pancakes or several tablespoonfuls for smaller portions. Press down to make a flat, even cake. Cook for about 2 minutes on each side or until pancakes are well-browned and cooked through. Sauté in batches and add oil as needed. Serve immediately.

MAKES 6 LARGE PANCAKES

Kitchen Wisdom

My colleague Maiken Scott came up with the ingenious idea of using a salad spinner to drain the grated potatoes.

Blini

Travel can be a recipe rescuer's best, and most fun, technique. There's nothing to compare to learning how to make an authentic dish in a foreign land. When my son, Ben, traveled to St. Petersburg, Russia, his host mother, Tatyana, made these blini almost every day for breakfast and served them with homemade blackberry jam and sour cream. I requested the recipe and received periodic updates on the cooking lessons and the hilarious Russian-English attempts at clarity.

Tatyana made these in a cast-iron pan that was passed down from her grandmother to her mother, as was the pancake technique. I was curious why Tatyana goes the extra step of mixing the batter in two parts. Ben wisely informed me that you never argue with a home cook who's done this thousands of times, no matter on what continent she resides.

I was surprised to learn that these were made with white flour rather than buckwheat flour. Oddly enough, Ben never encountered a blini made with buckwheat in St. Petersburg, nor could he find the word in his dictionary to ask. In Hungary these pancakes are called *palacsinta*.

2 cups whole milk	2½ cups flour
3 eggs	vegetable oil (not olive oil), for frying
½ cup warm water	good-quality jam and sour cream, for
¼ cup sugar	serving
1 teaspoon salt	

In a large bowl, whisk milk, eggs, and water. Add sugar and salt and mix well. Set aside half the mixture (about 1⅓ cup).

Add flour, a little at a time, whisking constantly until it is thick and spongy. Whisk in reserved egg mixture until it is smooth and has no lumps.

Heat a 9-inch cast-iron skillet until it is very hot. Add about 2 tablespoons oil and swirl it around. Pour off excess. Reduce heat to medium low.

Tilt pan, quickly pour a scant ¼ cup of the batter and swirl it around to coat the bottom. Cook for about 30 seconds or until the top bubbles slightly and turns a darker color. Flip and cook the second side for about 10 to 15 more seconds. Remove and continue cooking the remaining batter in this manner, using more oil as necessary. Stack blini on a plate.

To serve, fold blini into quarters and garnish with jam and sour cream.

MAKES ABOUT 16

Kitchen Wisdom

Tatyana says to decrease the sugar to one tablespoon to make blini for more savory dishes. During the long summer white nights, she often served blini with chopped tomato, dill, cucumber, and scallions. In the cafes, you'll find blini served with ground pork or beef and gravy. And, of course blini go well with caviar.

Dutch Pancake

I first saw this style of pancake in the seventies in a magazine that was originally called *Sphere,* which was later renamed *Cuisine.* Long before lifestyle magazines were invented—in fact, the November 1978 issue helped introduce Martha Stewart—this publication presented "fine food and creative living." Although the magazine ceased publication in the early eighties, I still enjoy all my back issues and cull through them when looking for recipes.

This is my own version of this versatile dish, which can be served with a filling as heartier fare. This simpler presentation makes a fine dessert or a breakfast item. It is very close to a popover, but much easier to prepare. Come to think of it, Dutch pancakes aren't too far removed from Yorkshire pudding.

2 eggs, beaten	2 tablespoons butter, cut in pieces
½ cup milk	½ lemon or lime
½ cup flour	2 tablespoons confectioners' sugar
¼ teaspoon salt	

Preheat oven to 425° F. Set an ovenproof 10-inch skillet on the lowest rack to heat up.

In a medium bowl, mix eggs and milk. Add flour and salt, whisking until blended. A few lumps are fine.

Using an oven mitt, remove the skillet from the oven and add butter pieces, tilting the pan until melted butter coats the bottom. Add batter and immediately return to oven. Bake for 15 to 20 minutes, or until puffy and browned. Squeeze lemon or lime juice over the top and dust with confectioners' sugar. Cut into 6 wedges and serve immediately.

MAKES 6 SLICES

HOME BEFORE DARK

*U*ntil I was eleven years old, my home was in a neighborhood of Akron, Ohio. We were middle-class kids, baby boomers born to parents home from World War II. Although still within city limits, the area hadn't yet been overdeveloped. We had a woods and a swamp to be kids in while our parents could feel postwar prosperity and ownership. We roamed from yard to yard—pretty much with abandon, or so we thought. One rule was consistent: home for dinner as soon as the street lights go on.

It was the fifties and the nuclear family held sway. Families sat down to dinner and ate home-cooked meals. Meat and potatoes were the operative words. Our parents, who had grown up during the Depression and entered adulthood during wartime rationing, took comfort in the bounty they provided. With "enough" regularly on the table, they turned their attention to manners, family conversation, and an attempt at creating a real Norman Rockwell scene.

In retrospect, those picture-perfect Norman Rockwell meals were a bit of an exaggeration and poetic license. That Thanksgiving dinner with smiling family members around Pops carving a plump bird with a red-haired boy sneaking a piece to the dog was a cute snapshot. My childhood dog, however, never stopped at a piece of drumstick. Entire pies would disappear without ever making it to the table. And forget leftovers if you didn't package everything up in the fridge moments after the meal.

It was precisely because of that food-stealing dachshund that I proclaimed I'd never own a dog as an adult. I finally ran out of excuses when my then eight-year-old son announced that "a boy without a dog is an unwritten story." Shortly after this, I succumbed and we adopted a two-year-old springer spaniel. We named him "Thurber"—after James Thurber's description of a lugubrious-looking spaniel who had the countenance of "a bachelor on his way to a party he has tried in vain to get out of…." Thurber seemed more in tune with my life than Rockwell, anyway.

I began to be won over to the idea of having a dog when I discovered Thurber was a gourmet dog. Oh sure, he might be tempted by an available garbage can, but for the most part his tastes ran to highly developed flavor systems and quality ingredients. Pavlovian response aside, the sight of my stockpot coming into view would bring spasms of joy. I've always made a lot of homemade soups— they are cheap to make, taste great, and infuse the house with an aroma that makes people happy to walk in the door. It seemed only fair to drizzle a little stock on Thurber's kibble. He expressed his appreciation by performing several pirouettes in a row when presented with his dish.

I hadn't realized the extent of his culinary acumen until one day when I returned home from my work in the test kitchen of a major corporation. A salesman had pressed me to try a sample packaged gravy mix. We rarely eat processed food in my house, but I thought I would sample a spoonful and dress Thurber's dinner with some of the excess.

Thurber saw the gravy being poured over the dish and the ritual began: up in the air with the power of Nureyev, full 360 rotation, barely a landing, and repeat the action two more times. As he jetéd toward the dish, his nose inches away, he got a look of disdain. All four paws splayed outward like a cartoon character and you could almost see "SCREECH" written underneath him. He stopped. Sniffed. He looked at me like a fastidious food critic presented with shelf-stable military K rations. In short, he refused to eat it (although this convenience product is used in many restaurants across the country).

For several days he gave me the cold shoulder for this transgression. I learned my lesson and never again tried to pass off anything I wouldn't eat myself. In return, he remained loyal to us for over ten years, always coming home before dark and giving each of us a story. To this day, whenever I make homemade soup I'm sure I'll see him trotting around the corner.

There are some aromas that stop us dead in our tracks with pleasant memories. In an instant, you return to a place in time. These are the dishes that greeted us after a spelling test, an afternoon of tag, or a hard day's work. They remind us of place, who we are, and why home beckons.

We walk in the door and are instantly comforted by the familiar: a noseful of heady garlic or the pungency of ginger. For some it is a basic meatloaf, oven-fried chicken, or gingerbread. For others it is an ethnic dish from Korea or Hungary and it becomes the second generation's window to the parent or grandparent who grew up in a different landscape. Imitation or restaurant food won't do. Only authentic home cooking will suffice.

Like a Norman Rockwell portrait, food can paint its own enduring image. Here's a palette of flavors to call you home to the table before dark.

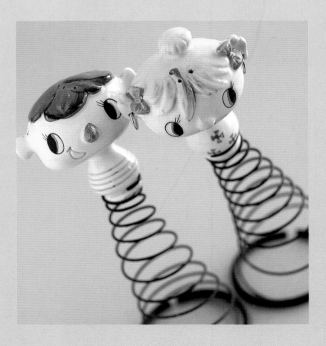

Tukare Pie

*T*his sausage pie is served at every Thanksgiving meal we share with our neighbor Terry Ruhl. Terry got the recipe from her friend's mother, Mrs. Holland, on one condition: the recipe was not to be shared with Mrs. Holland's children. Mom feared the only reason the kids came home for the holidays was for a taste of this pie and they wouldn't make the trip if they could make it for themselves. Terry kept the recipe secret but, being an enterprising person, years later she started a cottage industry selling these pies frozen for holiday entertaining. Advertising them as a Holland recipe handed down from generation to generation, customers began calling it Dutch pie, although the original recipe was from Mrs. Holland's French Canadian grandmother. Tukare seems to be an adaptation of *tourtiere,* a spicy pork pie served on Christmas Eve.

1 pound all-purpose white potatoes (2 to 3 medium), peeled and quartered

1 pound ground sausage meat, or link removed from casing

1 large onion, diced

8 ounces sharp cheddar cheese, grated

1 recipe Marie Dugan's Pie Crust (page 83), or your favorite pie crust

Preheat oven to 350° F.

In a medium pot, bring potatoes to a boil and simmer until tender, about 20 minutes.

Meanwhile, heat a medium skillet over medium heat. Crumble sausage into the pan and cook, stirring frequently, until no more pink remains. Add onion and continue cooking until onions are translucent and sausage is cooked through.

Remove sausage from pan and set aside, leaving excess drippings in pan. When potatoes are cooked through, peel and press through a ricer or mash with a fork. If they are dry, add a tablespoon or so of the cooking water. Toss potatoes and cheese with sausage.

Line a 9-inch pie pan with 1 round of unbaked pie crust and spoon in sausage mixture. Top with second round of pie crust and crimp edges.

Bake for 50 to 55 minutes, or until crust is browned. Remove and let sit for 15 minutes before cutting.

SERVES 6 TO 8

Kitchen Wisdom

This recipe lends itself to all kinds of flavors. Try hot Italian sausage with mozzarella and basil or Breakfast Sausage (page 65) with Gouda. It also is a great place for leftovers. Throw in a handful of leftover peas or carrots or use leftover mashed potatoes in the recipe.

Korean Steak on Fire (Bulgogi)

In Korea, beef is for special occasions. Mrs. Knapp remembers her mother making this almost every year for her birthday. Now it is the special dish all her grown children request when they return home for a visit. Here in this country it is ideal for both special occasions and a quick everyday meal. One of the delights of this dish is how adaptable it is—pork and chicken are just as delicious as beef. Mrs. Knapp has even tried this with a splash of ginger ale in place of the fresh ginger. Bulgogi can also be grilled.

1½ to 2 pounds beef top round

½ cup thinly sliced scallions (about 5)

¼ cup soy sauce

⅓ cup toasted sesame oil

2 to 3 cloves garlic, finely minced

1 tablespoon freshly grated ginger (about 2 inches)

2 tablespoons canola oil

Slice the beef into strips no more than 2 inches long and ⅛ inch thick.

Combine scallions, soy sauce, sesame oil, garlic, and ginger and mix well. Pour over the meat, stirring well to coat every piece. Press a piece of plastic wrap over the top of the meat and refrigerate for 2 hours.

Heat a large skillet over high heat until almost smoking. Add canola oil and spread around the bottom of the pan. Add the beef by handfuls, stirring well. When the beef is just barely pink in the middle, remove the pan from the heat and serve immediately.

SERVES 4 TO 6

Farfel

In our predominately WASPY neighborhood in Akron, Ohio, I was lucky to live next door to Mrs. R and her tasty Jewish cooking. Whenever I would wander over—which was often—I was assured of having my cheeks pinched and my belly filled with something wonderful to eat. I loved this dish so much, I insisted my mother learn how to make it. It has a nutty taste and the noodles seem more like a grain than pasta. I've substituted fresh mushrooms for canned in the original recipe, but keep the condensed beef consommé. It somehow works best.

1 tablespoon butter, plus more for
   dotting casserole, if desired
½ cup diced onions
1½ cups thinly sliced mushrooms

2 10-ounce cans condensed beef
   consommé, undiluted
1 12-ounce package toasted egg
   barley noodles

Preheat oven to 350° F.

In a large skillet, melt butter over medium-high heat. Add onions and sauté until translucent. Add mushroom slices and cook until mushrooms begin to lose their liquid.

Combine onion, mushrooms, consommé, and noodles in a 1-quart covered baking dish. For a richer dish, dot the casserole with additional butter. Bake for 1 hour or until pasta is cooked through and broth has been absorbed.

MAKES 4 CUPS

Oven–Fried Chicken

*W*e used this method of "frying" when I was growing up. Rather than cleaning the fryer and dealing with oil, oven-baked chicken was considered a convenience. I don't think it was a matter of health, because we still managed to dump a lot of butter on the meat. I've found I can eliminate the butter and still get a crispy coating. Try substituting Cajun seasoning for the paprika, or sweet paprika if you don't want the heat. The packaged oven-fried chicken product that came out in the sixties is not only more expensive, but also not nearly as flavorful. The TV commercial, however, remains in our cultural lexicon and we can all say, "And I helped."

1 cup cornflake crumbs

1 tablespoon hot paprika

½ teaspoon salt

1 egg white, beaten until frothy

3 pounds chicken pieces

5 tablespoons butter, melted (optional)

Preheat oven to 400° F.

On a large plate, mix together cornflakes, paprika, and salt. Put egg white on another plate.

Dip chicken pieces in beaten egg white and then in cornflake mixture. Coat thoroughly and set on a shallow baking sheet. Drizzle with butter, if desired. Bake for 1 hour or until juices of the chicken run clear.

SERVES 4 TO 6

Kitchen Wisdom

Before convenience products took over, home cooks often made their own mixes. By combining the dry ingredients ahead of time and storing them in a glass jar, the breading was ready for chicken, steak, or pork chops.

Noodles and Cabbage

*R*ozanne Gold is a magnificent professional chef. Her family background is Hungarian, and she grew up on substantial foods such as this dish. Today Rozanne is known for her three-ingredient recipes (not counting salt, pepper, and water) which bring quality ingredients together with such simplicity that the dish becomes more than the sum of its parts. One day I had the pleasure of joining Rozanne and her beautiful mother, Marion, in the kitchen to cook some of her childhood dishes. We were surprised when we realized that this is a classic example of a three-ingredient recipe. The taste is amazingly complex.

1 large cabbage (about 2½ pounds), quartered and cored
¼ cup kosher salt
7 tablespoons unsalted butter

12 ounces cooked double egg noodle twists
freshly ground black pepper

Slice cabbage into ¼-inch shreds. Place it in a large colander and sprinkle salt evenly over all on top, toss well. Cover with a plate to weight it down, putting a heavy object on top. Set aside for 3 to 4 hours.

Rinse and drain the cabbage, squeezing it dry with your fists to extract as much water as possible.

Melt butter in a large skillet until it just begins to bubble. Add cabbage. Keep careful watch and stir frequently for 30 to 40 minutes, until cabbage is a deep golden brown. Reduce heat, if necessary, to prevent the cabbage from burning.

Cook noodles in a large pot of boiling, salted water, until just tender, about 15 minutes. Drain thoroughly and place in a warm bowl. Add the hot cabbage and toss together so that the noodles are incorporated with the cabbage. Add lots of freshly ground black pepper.

SERVES 4

Kitchen Wisdom

Marion says the cabbage can be frozen after it has been cooked to a deep golden brown. A quick thaw and preparation of the pasta is all that is required to bring the dish to the table. Make a batch to reserve for company, or serve half now and freeze half for a busy family night.

Recipe Rescuer Sandy Oliver

A shawl is neatly draped over Sandy Oliver's shoulders and a few wisps of hair fall from her Gibson girl bun. It's hard to believe a woman who looks like a 19th-century portrait helped convince an international company to reverse a decision. But that she did.

"Well, at first I didn't notice that it had gone missing," recalls Sandy. "Then I got a call that Crown Pilot crackers weren't being made anymore."

Sandy is a food historian. She edits and publishes *Food History News*, a quarterly newsletter. Her book, *Saltwater Foodways*, won a Julia Child cookbook award for scholarship. When word came of the cracker's demise, Sandy got busy.

She found out that this is a familiar saga in our culinary evolution today. Regional products are a difficult fit with a major corporation's global sales and projections. Smaller markets don't have the capacity to make a large impact on quarterly sales reports. In a corporation's view, it simply isn't worth the effort to try for a piece of a small pie when the Guinness-book-of-records-size pie can be had.

Crown Pilot crackers, long a staple of New England chowders, fit into this category. The cracker has an interesting history, having been purchased from a Massachusetts business over a century ago by Nabisco. Says Sandy, "This is Nabisco's oldest recipe, but in recent years the cracker didn't meet product sales goals."

It was not necessarily that the cracker wasn't profitable, Sandy notes. The problem was that it couldn't meet the aggressive goals for sales growth of a megacorporation. She explains, "It's like asking an eighty-five-year-old man to get out and finish a marathon with twenty-year-olds. He can finish the course, but not in the same amount of time."

Sandy and other interested parties started a letter-writing campaign to Nabisco. Then the campaign came to the attention of the TV show *CBS Sunday Morning*. A feature on the show got a lot of food people worked up and the little cracker that couldn't suddenly could. Nabisco relented and started manufacturing them again.

Even though one of the sites where they are made is a factory in Philadelphia, I can't go to my neighborhood store and buy them. Today Crown Pilots are made by Nabisco and sold in New England or on the Internet, but wider distribution is unlikely.

For Sandy it is a small victory in a sea of losses. She says, "So many people think cooking is just what they see in the slick gourmet magazines." Instead, Sandy sees the historical link between what we eat today and our history slipping away. The loss of the cracker would be one more piece of our foodways to become extinct.

The recipe for New England chowder had its beginnings on the high seas where seafarers' provisions such as salt pork and hardtack were boiled with fresh fish heads. It came ashore in the 18th century and potatoes were added. Then in the 19th century, when milk was added, the chowder became the dish we know today. The greatest triumph for Sandy, though, was when the CBS story aired showing Sandy in her kitchen making the dish. A colleague's crusty Maine father was heard to mutter, "It's nice to see somebody still knows how to make a propah chowdah."

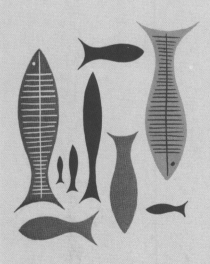

New England Fish Chowder

*S*andy notes that the whole point of chowders is that they don't require recipes. Instead, she figures on a formula per person: one quarter-pound of fish, one medium potato, half a medium onion, one cracker, and enough liquid to float 'er. Once you have the basics down you can change some of the quantities depending on what's on hand—adding or subtracting a potato and using whatever good white fish is available. The Crown Pilot crackers, however, are an essential ingredient (see appendix page 187 for ordering information) and become very dumpling-like in the broth. This soup will definitely bring you home. For those who require a recipe, Sandy offers the following.

2-inch-square piece salt pork, finely chopped

2 medium onions, cut in half lengthwise and thinly sliced crosswise

1 pound cod, cut into 1-inch pieces (may substitute haddock, cusk, or hake)

4 medium potatoes, peeled and sliced

3 to 4 Crown Pilot crackers, broken into 1- or 2-inch pieces

about 1 quart water

1 12-ounce can evaporated milk

Render the salt pork in a large heavy-bottomed pot. Layer in onions, cod, potatoes, and crackers loosely so that you can see the previous layer.

Add 1 quart water or enough to cover until it just appears among the ingredients. Bring to a boil. Reduce the heat, cover, and simmer for about 30 minutes, or until the potatoes are soft.

Add the evaporated milk and heat it through. (Sandy notes to stir and heat "gently, gently.") If desired, serve the chowder with a pat of sweet butter on top.

MAKES ABOUT 8 CUPS

Easy Biscuits

$\mathscr{I}$ found this recipe in one of my mother-in-law's church cookbooks, *The Pantry Shelf* by members of Indianapolis Christian School. The school kindly gave me permission to reprint the recipe here. You might ask, why not just use a biscuit mix? Try these and you'll know. They come out lighter and more tender, without that acrid taste of baking powder that so many biscuit mixes have. And these are far superior to the biscuits that come in a can.

This recipe's convenient: it uses ingredients that are easy to find, it's quick to make, and it adapts to the demands of the moment. The biscuits can be sprinkled with cheese or herbs before baking, or be turned into a shortcake dessert by sprinkling with sugar and cinnamon. These also make wonderful little finger sandwiches with ham, prosciutto, or smoked turkey.

1 cup self-rising flour

1 cup sour cream

Preheat oven to 425° F.

In a medium bowl, blend sour cream and flour together with a fork until it just comes together.

On a well-floured board, roll out dough to ¾-inch thickness. Using a floured 1-inch biscuit cutter, cut out 12 rounds, reworking the dough as little as possible.

Place biscuits on a greased cookie sheet and bake in the top third of the oven for 12 to 15 minutes, or until biscuits are lightly brown.

MAKES ABOUT 1 DOZEN

Tomato Soup

Too many condensed, canned versions of tomato soup have made this an endangered recipe. In the summer, make it with fresh peeled, seeded, and chopped plum tomatoes. And in that case, because it is summer, you might just want to serve it chilled, with a little dollop of sour cream or yogurt. I like to pair this with Welsh Rarebit (page 107) for an upscale grilled cheese sandwich and tomato soup combo.

1 medium carrot

1 large rib celery

1 medium onion

1 stick (4 ounces) butter or ½ cup
    olive oil

1 tablespoon flour

1 26-ounce can chopped tomatoes
    (about 3 cups)

1 cup chicken broth or water

2 bay leaves

½ teaspoon salt

⅛ teaspoon black pepper

1 cup whole milk

croutons, preferably whole wheat, for
    serving

Cut carrot, celery, and onion into large chunks and process in a food processor until finely grated.

In a medium saucepan, heat butter over medium heat and cook vegetables until soft and translucent, about 3 to 4 minutes. Add flour and cook until flour is absorbed, about 1 minute.

Add tomatoes, broth, bay leaves, salt, and pepper. Simmer soup uncovered over low heat for 30 minutes, stirring occasionally. Let cool. Remove bay leaves. Using a blender, food processor, or immersion blender, process until smooth. For best texture, strain through a medium-mesh strainer or china cap.

Stir in milk. Gently heat through. Serve, garnished with croutons.

MAKES 1 QUART OR 4 TO 6 SERVINGS

Gingerbread

*T*his should be named Goldilocks Gingerbread. When I set out to find my childhood version of gingerbread, I couldn't find one that measured up to memory. It seems no one had a recipe for the after-school treat I recalled—a light cake that was tall and moist with a very thin crusty skin on top and just enough spice. I would find a recipe for gingerbread that was too small, too spicy, or too dense. Finally after many tests, this one is just right. I like to use an eight-inch pan because I like the final product to be quite tall. Pans vary, so if your pan doesn't accommodate all the batter, use a slightly larger one.

2½ cups flour

1 teaspoon cinnamon

1 teaspoon ginger

¾ teaspoon baking powder

¾ teaspoon baking soda

½ teaspoon ground cloves

¾ cup boiling water

1½ sticks (6 ounces) butter, cut into
   small pieces

¾ cup sugar

¾ cup light molasses (see Kitchen
   Wisdom on page 152)

2 eggs, beaten

Preheat oven to 350° F. Spray an 8-inch square baking pan with nonstick cooking spray.

In a medium bowl, combine flour, cinnamon, ginger, baking powder, baking soda, and cloves and set aside.

In a large bowl, pour boiling water over butter. Add sugar, molasses, and eggs. Beat well.

Add dry ingredients and mix well. Pour batter into the prepared pan and bake for 45 to 50 minutes, or until a toothpick inserted in the center comes out clean. Let cool slightly before cutting.

MAKES 9 GENEROUS SLICES

Kitchen Wisdom

When shopping for molasses remember there are several kinds. Many brands have different selections, depending on whether it comes from the first, second, or third boiling of the syrup made from sugarcane or sugar beets.

Most popular is light molasses. This is lighter in color and flavor and comes from the first boil. Dark molasses comes from the second boil and is not as sweet. Blackstrap molasses is thick, very dark, and has a bitter flavor. It is rarely used in baking, although some bakers like to use it for gingerbread houses. Many health-food aficionados note that blackstrap molasses is rich in calcium, iron, and potassium and recommend adding it to hot beverages.

Mend-a-Broken-Heart Brownies

When I was in college, I was madly in love with a young man. One of his favorite desserts was his mother's brownies. He didn't last, but the well-used card in my recipe box lasted for, well, let's just say several boyfriends and many more years. The beauty of this recipe is that it requires little effort and just a few staples from the pantry, making it an ideal quick salve for a disappointed heart or a welcome home. It's as easy as boxed mixes, but this homemade version tastes far superior.

4 tablespoons butter, cut in pieces	2 eggs
2 squares unsweetened chocolate	¾ cup flour
1 cup sugar	¼ teaspoon salt
½ teaspoon vanilla extract	1 cup toasted chopped nuts (optional)

Preheat oven to 350° F.

Melt butter and chocolate in a medium saucepan over low heat, stirring constantly. Beat in sugar and vanilla. Add eggs one at a time, beating well after each addition. Add flour and salt. Mix well and, if desired, add nuts.

Pour batter into a greased 8-inch square baking pan. Bake for 25 to 30 minutes, or until firm and a toothpick inserted in the center comes out clean. Do not overbake.

MAKES 9 2½-INCH BROWNIES

Kitchen Wisdom

In a pinch you may substitute six tablespoons cocoa and two additional tablespoons of butter for the chocolate.

Triple-Sin Brownies

One of the enjoyable aspects of recipe rescuing is discovering how many different ways there are to make one dish. This chunky brownie was my signature dessert when I had a catering business. The brownies are so sinful they almost destroyed a customer's marriage. On a long trip the driver passed her brownie over to her husband with the request to "please hold this." When she went to get her brownie back, it had been consumed. Words ensued. Now, at least that is the version that I heard. I'll stop there lest I hear that an anecdote in my book caused further marital discord. The three sins are, of course, chocolate in three forms.

1⅓ cups flour	1 teaspoon vanilla extract
½ cup unsweetened cocoa powder	1 tablespoon crème de cacao
¼ teaspoon salt	½ cup toasted hazelnuts, chopped
2 sticks (½ pound) butter	1 ounce semisweet chocolate, cut into
1⅓ cups sugar	chunks (¼ cup)
2 eggs	

Preheat oven to 350° F. Spray an 8-inch square baking pan with nonstick cooking spray.

In a medium bowl, sift or blend together flour, cocoa, and salt. Set aside.

In a large bowl, cream butter and sugar. Add eggs one at a time, beating well after each addition. Add flour mixture to butter mixture and beat well. Add vanilla and crème de cacao. Mix well. Blend in nuts and chocolate.

Pour the batter into the prepared pan and bake for 45 to 50 minutes, until a toothpick inserted in the center comes out clean.

MAKES 9 GENEROUS BROWNIES

Rugalach

*F*resh out of graduate school, I had a job for which I was singularly unsuited. I was a rehabilitation teacher for visually impaired senior citizens. It was around that time when a young woman's options were to be a teacher or a nurse and, most certainly, not a chef. While teaching the use of script-writing devices I would assign my students the task of recording a recipe. This, despite my incompetence, at least gave us something to talk about and, because this was New York City, greatly enlarged my midwestern palate.

One of my favorite students gave me a rugalach recipe almost identical to this, but without the sugar. Recently, Arlene Miller gave me her family's version, which is essentially the same, but with the addition of the confectioners' sugar. I think the sugar makes these melt in your mouth. Poppy seed paste or a mixture of cinnamon sugar, walnuts, and dried fruit are also traditional fillings.

2 sticks (½ pound) butter, at room temperature and cut into pieces
½ pound cream cheese, at room temperature
1 teaspoon vanilla extract

2 cups flour
½ cup confectioners' sugar, plus some for garnish
⅔ cup apricot jam, for filling

In an electric mixer, blend butter, cream cheese, and vanilla until well mixed and smooth. In a medium bowl, mix flour and sugar together and add to butter mixture. Mix just enough to come together in a ball. Wrap in plastic wrap and refrigerate the dough for a few hours or overnight.

Preheat oven to 350° F. Line a cookie sheet with parchment paper.

Divide the dough in half. On a lightly floured board, roll 1 dough half into a 12-by-12-inch square, about ⅛ inch thick. For large cookies, cut into 4-inch squares; for small, cut into 3-inch squares.

Place a teaspoon of jam on a corner of one of the squares. Roll up the dough to the diagonal corner and make a crescent. Seal the ends and place on the prepared pan. Bake for 20 to 25 minutes, or until a golden brown. When cooled, dust with additional confectioners' sugar.

MAKES 18 LARGE OR 32 SMALL COOKIES

Kitchen Wisdom

A good dough is great to have. This rich, flaky dough doesn't have to be reserved for sweets. Try your hand at making some savory hors d'oeuvres by substituting blue cheese, spiced nuts, or even a little chopped chicken liver for the filling. Discover where your inspiration can take you.

Dog Biscuits

$\mathcal{A}$ little stock from the soup pot may wag a tail, but there's nothing like a home-made dog biscuit to call your pet home. My many pooch taste testers agree. Our neighbor Aspen, a golden retriever with a picky appetite, chose these over her favorite name-brand treat. Instead of making biscuits, you can also roll the dough into logs and cut into bite-size treats for training exercises. Unfortunately, that doesn't work for my current dog, Tennessee, because she gets so excited by these treats she can't concentrate on the task at hand. Children do enjoy making these, but be sure to also make a "people treat" at the same time!

1 cup beef broth

¼ cup peanut butter

2 tablespoons olive oil

1½ cups white flour

1 cup whole wheat flour

¼ cup wheat germ

¼ cup cornmeal

Preheat oven to 350° F.

Mix broth, peanut butter, and olive oil together. Add remaining ingredients, and mix into a smooth dough.

Roll out about ½ inch thick and cut to desired shape with a biscuit cutter. Bake for 20 minutes or until browned. Remove from oven and let cool.

For a crunchier treat, microwave 3 to 4 biscuits at a time for about a minute to a minute and a half. Let cool. Store in an airtight jar.

MAKES ABOUT 2 DOZEN 4- TO 5-INCH BONES

BACK PORCH PLEASURES

$\mathcal{F}$ront porches are for show. They are white wicker, swings, and Martha Stewart. Front porches are meant for first impressions rather than lingering. Front porches brag. They are studied and meant for campaign promises. You won't find easy living on a front porch.

Back porches, on the other hand, are for pleasure. They need paint and, more often than not, the furniture is for comfort, rather than looks. Back porches are meant for solitude or communion. It's where you go to read a trashy novel, watch a sunset, or engage in idle chatter. It's where a child learns to blow bubbles and watch for shooting stars. Old dogs—always positioned most inconveniently on the top step—dream of younger days. There's a timelessness to back porches.

The ideal back porch is large enough to accommodate a fair number of people, but not so big and open an expanse as to preclude being lazy and indolent in private. It should be well-worn, but not in need of major repairs or chores that guilt you out of that recliner. There should be steps, if for no other reason than one can impose a hierarchy of dominance when a crowd is arranging their behinds on every available space. The aesthetics of porch furniture is up to you, but I personally draw the line at anything stuffed that had a previous life in a family room. A boombox will suffice for music, but far better is an accomplished group of musicians who are hungry enough to play for their dinner.

What are fitting back porch activities? Home cooking and eating, of course. Simple ingredient preparation—such as shucking corn, stringing beans, or shelling peas—does best outdoors. Conversation definitely. Politics only if food is involved and not so much as to disrupt digestion. Checkers is an ideal sport, but a Game Boy should be banished like red dye #2.

A child who has not experienced hand-cranked ice cream on a back porch is deprived and most likely an impatient surly sort. Grabbing a carton of B&J out of the freezer might be immediate and convenient, but cranking your own ice cream and learning to be patient are life lessons.

The young person in question starts out cranking and it is easy, but as the cream thickens it becomes more difficult both physically and mentally. Just when she thinks she can do this no more, someone shares the task. When it seems as though sweet success is unattainable, the paddle comes out laden with a frozen confection. The children have learned the science of transformation, and discovered the reward of communal work and perseverance. And if you have done it correctly you, the adult, have imparted this lesson from a hammock with a cold drink in hand.

I discovered that in my neighborhood of century-old row houses, the back porch was the kitchen. Each house had two kitchens: one inside for cool seasons and a second summer kitchen on the porch to keep the heat of cooking out of the house. Nowadays most of the summer kitchens have been renovated to expand the first kitchen or, because of their sorry state, ripped off along with the privy that was usually attached. In the latter case, the space is often terraced and continues to function as a back porch.

Architecture aside, back porch living is becoming extinct. Busy lives take us away from home, but a little time on a back porch provides a space to reenergize. Certainly, a metaphoric back porch will suffice. It can be a park bench or picnic area in a public space. Or it can even be a state of mind—a commitment to spend time with yourself or loved ones with no agenda.

Food is a way to tell your story—whether you came from another country recently or the family has crisscrossed the country for generations. Does knowing exactly how Great Granny made peach ice cream for your mother when she was your age make it taste better? Does bringing a family tradition to another country keep you closer to those that stayed behind? I would emphatically say yes. Should we save endangered recipes? Again, an emphatic yes. Otherwise, we lose a piece of who we are.

These recipes are meant for casual living and outdoor dining. Slow down, sit down, sip a bit, and enjoy back porch pleasures.

Grilled Chicken Wings

These are better than Buffalo wings, although these also come from western New York State. When I worked at Chautauqua Institute one college summer, chicken cooked with this sauce was a popular item at summer parties on Lake Chautauqua. Unlike tomato-based grilling sauces, the sauce used here doesn't burn as easily. You can cook any chicken part with this sauce, but I'm fond of the wings done this way. They are even good cold the next day and perfect for porch sitting without having to cook.

2 egg yolks

⅓ cup vinegar (cider, malt, rice, or herbal is best)

2 tablespoons kosher salt

1 to 2 teaspoons water

12 chicken wings

Preheat a grill.

In a small bowl, beat egg yolks until creamy. Add vinegar and salt and beat until well mixed. Add enough water to make a thin sauce.

Grill wings over white coals, about 4 minutes per side. When the chicken is almost cooked, about 8 minutes, baste with the sauce. Turn the chicken often and remove from direct heat if flare-ups occur. The sauce will cook and form a nice crust. Chicken is done when the juices run clear.

SERVES 4

Grilled Salmon

*T*his combination of brown sugar and fish seems improbable, but it is delicious. The sugar, butter, and natural oil of the fish caramelize and bring out the sweetness of the salmon. I've even made this recipe inside on a little electric grill when outdoor grilling wasn't an option. In Alaska, the butter and sugar combination is widely used for grilling salmon.

1 stick (4 ounces) butter, cut in pieces
1½ cups dark brown sugar
¼ cup lemon juice

½ teaspoon hot sauce
4 to 6 salmon steaks, 6–8 ounces each

Preheat a grill.

Mix all ingredients except the salmon in a small saucepan. Cook over low heat, stirring occasionally, until sugar is melted and the mixture forms a thick sauce.

On the well-oiled grill, cook salmon steaks over medium-high heat on one side for 2 to 3 minutes. Turn and baste. Flip over and cook the second side for 2 to 3 minutes; turn and baste.

Watch carefully and pull the steak away from direct heat if it flares up. Keep a watchful eye—the butter and sugar burn easily.

MAKES ABOUT ¾ CUP

Kitchen Wisdom

If the sauce becomes too cool, it will be difficult to spread. To keep it warm, place it off direct heat on the grill in a pan.

Potatoes and Peas in White Sauce

Shelling fresh peas is the ultimate back porch activity. Green peas, also known as English or spring peas, come in to season late spring and early summer when the excitement of warmer weather is at its peak. Shelling peas is a communal activity—living proof that many hands make light work. You'll also discover that there is something about shelling peas that is conducive to talking. All in all, it is a very pleasant activity. While you can use frozen peas, it just isn't the same experience.

1 pound small new potatoes or
    fingerlings, washed and scrubbed
2 cups freshly shelled green peas
    (from about 2 pounds whole peas)

1 tablespoon plus 2 teaspoons butter
1 tablespoon plus 2 teaspoons flour
1½ cups milk

With a vegetable peeler, remove a band of the skin from the middle of the potatoes.

In a medium saucepan, boil the potatoes until tender, 15 to 20 minutes. Drain.

In a medium saucepan, boil the peas until tender, 10 to 20 minutes depending on how fresh the peas are. Drain.

Meanwhile, prepare the white sauce by melting the butter in a small pan. Add the flour and cook, stirring or whisking constantly, until the mixture is bubbly all over and the flour is cooked. Slowly add the milk, whisking constantly to incorporate it. Cook over medium heat, whisking constantly, until the sauce is thickened. If it is ready before the vegetables, set aside, but stir occasionally to keep a skin from forming.

Mix the peas, potatoes, and sauce together in a pan. Simmer for 3 to 5 minutes until heated through. Serve immediately.

MAKES ABOUT 6 SERVINGS

Kitchen Wisdom

Back when all young girls took Home Economics in school, there were two tasks required for graduation: make a white sauce and sew an apron. Political correctness aside, I think it wasn't a bad idea, though it should have applied to boys, too! A straight stitch is good for mending and a good white sauce can help many a meal, too.

The technique is always the same: cook the flour in hot butter, whisk in the milk, and cook until thickened. Here are the proportions to make 1 cup:

THIN WHITE SAUCE

for cream soups and vegetables as well as a base for cheese sauce

1 tablespoon butter

1 tablespoon flour

1 cup milk

MEDIUM WHITE SAUCE

for meat and fish casserole dishes and for escalloped potatoes

2 tablespoons butter

2 tablespoons flour

1 cup milk

THICK WHITE SAUCE

for use as a binder in croquettes, fish cakes, and soufflés

3 tablespoons butter

3 tablespoons flour

1 cup milk

Quick Cinnamon Buns

*T*his recipe is easier than the long list of ingredients and instructions would imply. You can mix the dry ingredients the night before and quickly assemble these in the morning for a special breakfast treat on a sunny back porch.

BUNS

2 cups flour

1 tablespoon plus 1 teaspoon baking powder

1 tablespoon sugar

½ teaspoon salt

½ teaspoon cream of tartar

1 stick (4 ounces) butter

⅔ cup buttermilk

FILLING

3 tablespoons sugar

2 teaspoons cinnamon

¼ teaspoon nutmeg (or 12 good gratings of the nut)

¼ teaspoon cardamom (optional)

2 tablespoons melted butter

FROSTING

1 cup confectioners' sugar

1 tablespoon milk

1 teaspoon vanilla extract

Preheat oven to 425° F.

Make the buns: In a large bowl, mix flour, baking powder, sugar, salt, and cream of tartar. Cut in butter until the mixture resembles coarse crumbs. Slowly add buttermilk and gently mix with a fork until the dough comes together.

On a lightly floured board, knead dough gently to incorporate and make a ball. Do not overwork the dough or it will be tough.

Make the filling: In a small bowl, combine sugar, cinnamon, nutmeg, and cardamom, if using. Set aside.

Assemble the buns: Roll dough out to a 5- by 9-inch rectangle and generously brush the dough with the melted butter. Sprinkle filling over dough, leaving a ½-inch border. Drizzle remaining butter over filling.

Roll up the dough along the long side to make a log. Press the seam and ends together. Cut the log into 8 1-inch slices and place on an ungreased baking sheet about 1 inch apart. Bake for 12 to 15 minutes or until the buns are golden brown.

Make the frosting: Mix all the ingredients together in a small bowl.

When the rolls are done, drizzle frosting over the top of the buns. Save some frosting to serve on the side.

MAKES 8 BUNS

Kitchen Wisdom

To slice the log, it's easiest to cut the log in half, then cut each half in half, then cut each quarter in half. This way you are cutting the dough in the middle instead of the end, which helps keep the shape.

Nancy's Granny's Peach Ice Cream

I encountered this ice cream nearly thirty years ago at a party. I could taste that it was something special and sought out the person making it. We have been friends ever since. Nancy Ennis is an internationally exhibited artist and published author, and a fine recipe rescuer as well. Look for her Mustard Sauce (page 106). Granny was Nancy's paternal grandmother, Mary Simms Foley, from East Texas.

1 heaping quart peaches (about 2 pounds)

2½ cups sugar

1 quart heavy cream

3 cups light cream

2 tablespoons lemon juice

¼ teaspoon salt

Peel and pit peaches. Cut into 1-inch pieces and put in a large bowl. Mash well and blend in sugar.

Add remaining ingredients and mix well. Refrigerate until thoroughly chilled.

Pour the mixture into an ice cream maker and freeze according to the manufacturer's instructions.

MAKES ABOUT ½ GALLON

Kitchen Wisdom

Be sure to mash your fruit so that there are no large pieces left, or you will find frozen peach rocks in your ice cream. Nancy says that mangoes work very well in this recipe, too.

Black Cow

$\mathcal{M}$y grandmother used to make these for me and we would drink them on the hanging swing on her porch. Once I went East I discovered that this drink is the midwestern version of an egg cream, the New York City beverage that is made with a mixture of flavoring syrup, milk, and seltzer. There are some camps that claim a black cow is made with ice cream rather than milk, but then to me it's just a root beer float. If you can find sarsaparilla to replace the root beer, so much the better. If you add a squirt of chocolate syrup, you have a black cow with a sling of mud.

about ¼ cup canned evaporated milk

ice

about 1 cup root beer

In a tall glass, pour milk over ice. Add root beer. Stir until frothy.

MAKES 1 DRINK

Fruit Cordial

I recall a plum cordial coming to the table around holiday time in Ohio. This beverage is usually made from fruit that comes into season in late summer. That makes it ideal to "put by" when fruit is at its peak. I was surprised to see a similar recipe in a church cookbook from Cincinnati, but it certainly validates it as an Ohio concoction. Serve a little thimbleful after dinner or over ice with a splash of soda and fresh mint for a summer refresher.

1 pound fruit (damson plum, peach, or cherry)

1 bottle vodka or gin (750 ml)

2 cups sugar

Wash and dry fruit. Keep whole. Place fruit in a clean, glass gallon jar. Add vodka and sugar. Shake bottle and leave in a cool, dark place.

For the first week, shake the bottle every day or so until the sugar is dissolved. Continue steeping the fruit for another 3 months. Check occasionally and shake if there is sediment. The fruit should be all shriveled and the cordial aromatic and flavorful. Strain the liquid into clean bottles and store in the refrigerator or a cool cupboard.

MAKES ABOUT 5 CUPS

Kitchen Wisdom

This home brew decanted into a decorative bottle makes a pleasant gift around the holidays.

Lemonade

*O*ne of my favorite movie scenes is in the thriller *Witness*. Harrison Ford's character is hiding in an Amish community where he and a local widow dodge bullets as well as an attraction to one another. In a revealing scene, she hand squeezes fresh lemons and brings him a glass. He guzzles it, spilling lemonade down his cheeks, never noticing her look of horror. His excess reinforces his coming from "outside." Handmade lemonade is an act of love. It should be savored, slowly.

3 cups bottled water (or exceptionally good tap water)

1 cup sugar

1 cup freshly squeezed lemon juice (from about 5 to 6 lemons)

In a medium saucepan, heat water and sugar just to a boil, stirring to dissolve the sugar.

Remove from heat and let cool.

Stir in the lemon juice. Taste, adding a little more water if it is too strong.

MAKES ABOUT 1 QUART

Kitchen Wisdom

Whenever you add sugar to a drink, a simple syrup is the way to go. It's handy for other uses, too. Boil the water and add the sugar, stirring to dissolve. Remove from the heat and let cool. To make a thin syrup, use three parts water to one part sugar (used in drinks or as a basis for other syrups); medium syrup, two parts to one (used in drinks or for soaking and glazing cakes); heavy syrup, one to one (used in preserving fruits or making candy).

Recipe Rescuer Luca Sena

Philadelphia's Italian Market is busy in the Christmas season, but it is festive and there is a lot of camaraderie among the merchants. My son, who works in the Market, came home late with the explanation that his colleagues had gotten together in the warehouse for "lemon Jell-O." This confused me. I didn't understand why young men would waste their precious time off eating a kid's dessert.

Some time later I discovered that what Ben was saying was "limon-cello" (pronounced like the instrument). This potent after-dinner cordial is made in nearly every southern Italian home and is particularly pleasant following a heavy meal. I also discovered most limoncello recipes are as secret as Hannibal's campaign across the Alps.

Happily, about the time that I discovered limoncello was not gelatin in a box, I met Luca Sena. He's from Naples, Italy, and is a third-generation restaurateur. He brings many of the customs and foods of his Italian heritage to Ristorante Panorama in Philadelphia. Panorama has won international acclaim for its wine bar which, due to a sophisticated preservation system, offers an array of wines by the glass. But you can also get a glass of Luca's mother's limoncello, served in a frosty shot glass and made just the way it has been for generations. Well, almost the same. Luca confesses he uses a few more lemons.

"You can't go wrong by having more lemons," he says. "Don't tell my mother I said that."

I suspect that is a bigger secret than Hannibal's!

Luca's Limoncello

*I*n southern Italy, a small, icy cold glass of limoncello is served after dinner as a *digestivo* to aid digestion. It is also available commercially—perhaps the best-known brand is Limoncello Liquore made in Capri. The best limoncello is still from a homemade family recipe. Look for thick-skinned, unblemished lemons of good quality such as Israeli lemons. If you can't find organic lemons, be sure to scrub your lemons well with baking soda. Juice the naked lemons and reserve for Lemonade (page 172) or baking.

12 to 14 high-quality lemons

1 liter grain alcohol (such as Everclear)

5 cups water

3½ cups sugar

Wash and dry lemons. With a vegetable peeler, peel off the lemon rinds into thin strips so that there is no white pith. In a 1-gallon glass or other nonreactive container, add alcohol and lemon peels. Let steep in a cool place for 7 days.

When peels have finished steeping, bring water to boil in a large saucepan. Add sugar and mix well to make a simple syrup. Let cool.

Blend simple syrup and alcohol together. Strain peels and pour liquid into a bottle. Store in the freezer. It's best if it cures for at least 2 weeks or more for a smoother flavor. Serve icy cold directly from the freezer.

MAKES ABOUT 2 QUARTS

Kitchen Wisdom

In some states, grain alcohol is not available. Sometimes a neutral spirit such as vodka can be substituted, but it does not bring out the lemon flavor and has a less desirable taste.

Hot Chocolate

$\mathcal{R}$ecipe rescuer and Native American chef Loretta Barrett Oden reminded me that it was the Olmec people of southern Mexico who discovered the complicated process of turning cocoa beans into chocolate over three thousand years ago. The Aztecs and Mayans came next and added their take. Most people think of hot chocolate as a winter drink. I like it in the fall when the nights are just beginning to chill. We sip it in the yard, aware that the days in our outdoor space are limited.

After you consume homemade hot chocolate, you'll never go back to the instant cocoa powder beverage. This is absolutely scrumptious served with plain Marshmallows (page 84) and a little sprinkling of cocoa powder. You may double or triple the recipe.

1 ounce unsweetened chocolate	**2 cups whole milk**
2 tablespoons sugar, or to taste	**¼ teaspoon vanilla extract**

In a medium saucepan, melt chocolate over low heat. Stir in sugar and mix well. Whisking constantly, add milk and cook over low heat until warmed through. Remove from heat and stir in vanilla. Serve immediately in warm mugs.

MAKES 2 CUPS

Kitchen Wisdom

Adding cold milk to the chocolate can sometimes cause it to seize up and become difficult to blend. Mixing in a little hot water with the chocolate before adding the milk will solve that problem, or you can make the drink in a double boiler.

PASSING DOWN THE PLATE

Collecting Your Own Family Recipes

The best way to begin collecting treasured family recipes is to just get into the kitchen. An actual written recipe from the original cook's hand is a good start. Better still, ask that cook to show you how to make the dish. You'll learn a lot about the recipe and the person. Otherwise, looking in old cookbooks for a recipe similar to the one you remember can start you on a fun project. In short, a recipe rescuer is a detective, genealogist, and historian.

Everyone knows the story of the family that made an Easter ham by cutting off the shank portion before roasting. Finally someone asked Mom why she did that and her response was "because your grandmother did it." When Grandma was asked, her answer was that her pan was too small to accommodate the whole ham. Although they had a bigger pan, the succeeding generations cut off the shank because that's what they knew. An exaggerated story perhaps, but there's a certain element of truth that some of what goes on in the kitchen is habit.

The passage of time may make a small pan dictate how to bake a ham, but time has also changed our ingredients. Remember when a one-pound coffee can was one pound? That was before companies decided we'd never miss a half ounce of coffee, but multiply that by millions and they'd instantly increase their profits. Whenever I find a real one-pound can of coffee, I buy a bunch because there are many recipes that call for a one-pound can as a mold. Ingredients and package sizes will change over the years, so be aware of that when reading hand-me-down recipes.

Some things have changed just because things change. Back when gas stoves were replacing wood-burning stoves, many cooks thought gas stoves just didn't cook as well. No doubt, hearth cookers found the newfangled wood burners less than desirable. So here we are with microwaves, convections, and even induction! Adjust the recipe for your appliance, but make sure you note for future generations exactly what you did. Who knows what they'll be cooking on? I have several handwritten recipes from my mother that have the temperature crossed out several times. We moved every few years and the oven temperature in each house was always plus or minus about 50 degrees. Individual oven thermostats can be off by as much as 100 degrees.

Recipe rescuer Lynn Nusom was once asked what to do when a dish just didn't come out. His astute advice? Throw it out! Seriously, there is nothing wrong with cooking a dish that is inedible. We've all done it. Granted it's more painful when the ingredient is $20 worth of cod than $2 worth of yeast and flour. All in all, that old axiom is true—you learn more from your mistakes. Go back over your notes and see if you can figure out what went wrong. I generally attempt a recipe three times, incorporating changes each time. If it's not working by then it's unlikely it will.

Here's a guide to rescuing your own family recipe treasures.

Cultivating Your Family Tree of Recipes

- Be a sleuth. After you've exhausted all your family sources, try local street festivals and bake sale tables. Look for recipes similar to the ones you remember. Ask questions—you'll make some wonderful discoveries.
- Record family anecdotes and memories with your recipes to make a culinary genealogy. There also may be some clue about the recipe hidden in the story, such as the fact that the original recipe came from Denver. Bingo—high altitude and that changes cooking time.
- Send completed recipes to other family members or friends. Consider setting up a family Web site with a recipe section. Keep the traditions alive.

Planning to Cook

- Sit down ahead of time and make a shopping and prep list. You'll need to know exact ingredients as well as what types of pans or special utensils are required.

- Ideally, plan a session when there are few distractions and plenty of time. It's not a good idea to try to learn how to make a five-layer chocolate cake when you are trying to get a holiday meal on the table.

Shopping for Ingredients

- Shop locally with small producers. You are more likely to get results similar to original recipes with products that are not mass-produced and are representative of the origin of the recipe. Also, buying locally from smaller producers helps keep them around for the next generation.
- Check sizes. Older recipes will call for items such as a tall can, a small can, or a large box of a particular name-brand ingredient. If you need clarification, try calling the company and ask if they have historical records to help you determine the specific volume. A recipe may give a specific number such as sixteen crackers, but who's to know that the size of the cracker hasn't changed? Buy extra in case you need more.

Recording the Recipe

- Assemble everything you need to make the dish ahead of time. Include plenty of notepaper and a back-up pen.
- List all ingredients in the order used and with standard measurements. If necessary, follow the original cook around the kitchen with liquid and dry measuring cups, measuring spoons, and ruler. Measure as much as you can before it is added. Get yields of batter before it is cooked. Too much information is better than not enough.
- Specify types of products needed such as unsalted butter or dark corn syrup.
- Use short sentences and simple directions. Make a note of how fast the boil is, the appearance of the batter, or the feel of a dough. These little details often mean the difference between success and so-so. Use qualifiers to help determine doneness or other elements of the recipe. For example: sauté onions until they begin to brown; bake until toothpick inserted in the center comes clean.
- Be specific about the pot or pan size and its composition—aluminum, glass, Teflon. Each will change cooking temperatures and times. Get a volume measurement (two-quart heavy saucepan) as well as dimensions (eight-inch square aluminum pan).

Retesting

- Rarely does a recipe work the first time. Even professional recipe testers will have to go back and adjust a recipe several times. Do research and look for similar recipes (also known as "mother" recipes). Look at the ratios of ingredients. For example, if you are making a cake and you find a similar recipe with one-half teaspoon baking power to two cups of flour and your recipe is one-half teaspoon to six cups of flour, you might extrapolate that your recipe should have read one-half tablespoon of baking powder—a likely typo if your cake didn't rise.

A Note on High-altitude Cooking

People who live in high altitudes know how to adjust their cooking. It can be tricky if you are trying to record a recipe that has been developed in a high altitude and you are cooking at sea level. Here are a few things to remember:

- The boiling point in higher altitudes is higher, so cooking times in high altitudes are longer. Shorten your cooking time for any food that is boiled or steamed.
- Deep-fried foods are cooked at a lower temperature in higher altitudes. Most foods are best fried at 375° F at lower altitudes.
- Yeast dough rises more rapidly at higher altitudes, so adjust the recipe for a longer rise.

Recording Recipes with Eggs

Egg sizes and equivalents can be very confusing when trying to re-create an older recipe. I used to think that egg sizes had gotten bigger because I no longer saw small eggs. Apparently, that's sort of chicken-and-egg thinking: it's not that small eggs no longer exist, but rather producers are sending small eggs to be further processed. Today 30 percent of eggs are used in products. When Grandma was on the farm, she used whatever size egg the hen laid and adjusted her recipe accordingly.

I also thought that retailers were cheating us in the spring around Easter because the eggs were visibly smaller when the demand was the greatest. I was half right. Yes, eggs look smaller in the spring. No, we are not being cheated! Eggs laid in the spring are smaller, but denser. Eggs are sized by weight, not volume—a large spring egg weighs the same as a large winter egg, although the spring egg will look smaller.

You probably won't go wrong purchasing large eggs for most recipes. The color of the eggshell makes no difference. My local farmers market has powder blue eggs, which I adore, but the performance and taste are the same.

The American Egg Board (www.aeb.org) provides this information:

Egg sizes are Jumbo, Extra Large, Large, Medium, Small, and Peewee. Medium, Large, and Extra Large are the sizes most commonly available.

Sizes are classified according to minimum net weight expressed in ounces per dozen.

Size Equivalents

Although any size egg may be used for frying, scrambling, cooking in the shell, or poaching, most recipes for baked dishes such as custards and cakes are based on the use of Large eggs. To substitute another size, use the following chart.

Size Equivalents

LARGE	JUMBO	X-LARGE	MEDIUM	SMALL
1	1	1	1	1
2	2	2	2	3
3	2	3	3	4
4	3	4	5	5
5	4	4	6	7
6	5	5	7	8

To Make 1 Cup

EGG SIZE	WHOLE	WHITES	YOLKS
Jumbo	4	5	11
X-Large	4	6	12
Large	5	7	14
Medium	5	8	16
Small	6	9	18

Chart and information used with permission of the American Egg Board

Candy Temperatures

You might run into a candy recipe or two while recording old recipes. Old family candy recipes can be delicious and fun to make. Here's a guide to help decipher them. There are two ways to determine what stage the candy is at: placing a spoonful in a glass of room-temperature water and observing the reaction or using a candy thermometer. Both methods are estimates. Experience is your best guide because elements such as humidity can affect the candy no matter what the temperature. While some cookbooks suggest using cold water for testing, a veteran candymaker in a generations-old candy store once instructed me that room-temperature water is the best because the candy needs to be stable at room temperature.

STAGE	DEGREES F	DESCRIPTION
thread stage	230–234	syrup spins a 2-inch thread when dropped from a spoon
soft ball	234–240	syrup dropped into water forms a soft ball which flattens when removed
firm ball	244–248	syrup dropped into water forms a firm ball which does not flatten when removed
hard ball	250–265	syrup dropped into water forms a ball which is hard enough to hold its shape
soft crack	270–290	syrup dropped into water separates into threads which are hard but not brittle
hard crack	300–310	syrup when dropped into water separates into threads which are hard and brittle
clear liquid	320	sugar liquefies
brown liquid	338	liquid becomes brown

Appendix

Deep-frying Technique

Over the past decade, we've been so fat phobic that the art of frying has virtually disappeared and needs to be rescued. Properly done, very little oil is absorbed by the food. I'm not claiming that this is health food to be consumed everyday, but far better to eat foods fried at home with the best ingredients, frying oil, and technique than to eat dough globs put out by the fast-food industry. There are some delicious recipes that use deep frying, so it is a technique worth learning. The Nashville House Fried Biscuits (page 34) recipe is a good start for the novice fryer.

I generally consider anything cooked in a fair amount of oil as frying. In other words, sautéing is technically frying. Pan frying gets the food in the hot oil, but doesn't cover it. Deep-fat frying is when the food is immersed in the oil, although as the food cooks it will float to the top and require turning.

There are some great books with far more information on frying than I can impart. If you want to be head fry cook read the chapter on frying in Alton Brown's *I'm Just Here for the Food* (Stewart, Tabori & Chang) or look at *The Fearless Frying Cookbook* by John Martin Taylor (Workman).

Whether deep frying or pan frying here are some keys to success:

- Get all your equipment out before you start. This includes tongs for turning, racks for draining, pot holders, and a frying thermometer.

- Choose your oil well. All things being equal, peanut oil or canola are the best because they have a higher smoke point (the temperature at which the oil begins to break down and therefore alter the taste of other foods). Look for non-hydrogenated oils, which are purer.

- Add only the appropriate amount of oil. If you add more, you could experience a dangerous boil over of the oil. Follow manufacturer's directions for appliances and never pour the pan more than half full with oil on stovetops.

- Keep your frying temperature between 325° F and 375° F. Never add too many food pieces at one time. This keeps the oil temperature from dropping and also helps avoid a boil over.

- Change the oil if you are frying in batches and there are any burned bits in the oil. You don't want to ruin a portion of the batch after having come this far!

- Generally speaking, if you use high-quality oil, you can cool, strain, and store the oil for use again. I never do this because I hate storing it and believe (true or not) that I can taste whatever was fried before. Since I don't fry that often, I allow myself this wastefulness. If you do choose to reuse oil, store in an airtight container away from air, heat, and light and give it up after three recycles.

Terminology Often Found in Older Recipes

BRAISE—cooking method applied to vegetables or meat in which the product is browned and then cooked, covered, with a small amount of liquid for a long time. The cooking can be stovetop or oven.

CRACKLINGS—little bits of skin that have been cooked in their own fat until very crisp. Cracklings can be used to garnish or flavor dishes. They are a favorite addition to cornbread.

DASH—a small measurement of a liquid, about six drops.

DRIPPINGS—the fats and juices released from meat as it cooks in a pan. These are often reserved for gravy or for use in another dish.

FRICASSEE—meat, usually chicken, that has been seared in butter and sautéed with vegetables so that the resulting dish is stewlike. The sauce may be thickened with egg yolks or a white sauce made with the stock.

MUTTON—meat from mature sheep (animal over two years of age), which needs a cooking technique to tenderize it. Substituting lamb (animal under one year of age) will mean a shorter cooking time.

OLEO—sometimes referred to as oleomargarine. It is synonymous with margarine, although the products out today are very different from the older versions. As late as 1967, due to the lobbying by the dairy industry, some states actually required that margarine be sold in its natural colorless condition. The white margarine came with yellow dye that the consumer could mix in. Some recipes will call for yellow or white oleo, but you may use one of today's margarine brands made for cooking. The dye does not affect taste.

OVEN TEMPERATURES
Slow oven 250–325° F
Moderate oven 325 to 375° F
Moderately hot oven 375 to 400° F
Hot oven 400 to 450° F
Very hot oven 450 to 500° F

PAN BROILING—cooking meat in a heavy pan over high heat using little or no added oil. Drippings are removed as soon as they accumulate.

PAN FRYING—similar to pan broiling, but there is a small amount of fat in the pan. This term is often used interchangeably with sautéing.

PINCH— small measurement of dry ingredient, ostensibly enough to grab between two fingers or, if you are on the rigid side, about one-eighth teaspoon or less.

POACH—cooking method applied to food cooked in a liquid but, unlike braising, not browned beforehand. The temperature of liquid is kept just below boiling. Poaching is a stovetop activity.

RENDER—cooking meat or animal fat until the fat melts.

SWEAT—a technique, usually applied to vegetables, in which the vegetables are covered and cooked with a small amount of fat over low heat until softened.

Food Sources and Informational Web Sites

www.bluechef.com

Jason Girard is the executive chef at Buddy Guy's Legends in Chicago. His recipes and cookbook, *The Blues Highways Cookbook,* records foods and stories of blues legends. Check out the BBQ links.

www.cheesemaking.com

Everything you need to have and need to know to make your own cheese.

www.cookswares.com

Source for packaged zahtar, a Lebanese spice blend. Or call 1 800-915-9788.

www.dibruno.com

Delicious Italian delicacies.

www.ethnicgrocer.com

Shop by country for hard-to-find ingredients.

www.foodhistorynews.com

Information about food history in North America edited by Sandra Oliver. Includes historic recipes, articles, and a yellow pages of products, services, and events.

www.foodroutes.org

Information on community sustainable agriculture.

www.fungi.com

Grow your own mushrooms indoors or out.

www.grits.com

Need I say more? Links to all things southern.

www.mechanical-bakery.com

Authentic hardtack source. Used by Civil War reenactors.

www.nativeseeds.org

Buy seed to grow as well as foods and crafts. Supports the preservation of Native American crop seeds.

www.netgrocer.com

Source for Nabisco Crown Pilot crackers used in Pensacola Gaspachee Salad (page 48) and New England Fish Chowder (page 146). Or call 1 800-622-4726.

www.noshnews.com

Information on New York City's ethnic neighborhoods for food shopping and dining.

www.rachelsimon.com/foodtogo.htm

Suggestions by Lari Robling for food on the road as inspired by Rachel Simon's book, *Riding the Bus with My Sister.*

www.taquitos.net

A fabulously fun Web site about snack foods.

www.whyy.org/chef

Web site for *A Chef's Table* radio show including Lari Robling's cookbook reviews and commentaries as well as recipes.

www.whyy.org/garden

Web site for *You Bet Your Garden* radio show with organic gardening tips.

Great Food Reads

The Art of Eating by M. F. K. Fisher. New York, NY: John Wiley and Sons, 1990 (reprint).

Best of Food Writing series edited by Holly Hughes. Emeryville, CA: Avalon Publishing Group.

Cornbread Nation 1: The Best of Southern Food Writing edited by John Egerton. Chapel Hill, NC: University of North Carolina Press, 2002.

Home Cooking: A Writer in the Kitchen by Laurie Colwin. New York, NY: Harper Collins, 2000 (reissue).

The Magic of Fire: Hearth Cooking by William Rubel. Berkeley, CA: Ten Speed Press, 2002.

Conversion Charts

Weight Equivalents

The metric weights given in this chart are not exact equivalents, but have been rounded up or down slightly to make measuring easier.

AVOIRDUPOIS	METRIC
¼ oz	7 g
½ oz	15 g
1 oz	30 g
2 oz	60 g
3 oz	90 g
4 oz	115 g
5 oz	150 g
6 oz	175 g
7 oz	200 g
8 oz (½ lb)	225 g
9 oz	250 g
10 oz	300 g
11 oz	325 g
12 oz	350 g
13 oz	375 g
14 oz	400 g
15 oz	425 g
16 oz (1 lb)	450 g
1½ lb	750 g
2 lb	900 g
2¼ lb	1 kg
3 lb	1.4 kg
4 lb	1.8 kg

Volume Equivalents

These are not exact equivalents for American cups and spoons, but have been rounded up or down slightly to make measuring easier.

AMERICAN	METRIC	IMPERIAL
¼ t	1.2 ml	
½ t	2.5 ml	
1 t	5.0 ml	
½ T (1.5 t)	7.5 ml	
1 T (3 t)	15 ml	
¼ cup (4 T) 60 ml	2 fl oz	
⅓ cup (5 T)	75 ml	2½ fl oz
½ cup (8 T)	125 ml	4 fl oz
⅔ cup (10 T)	150 ml	5 fl oz
¾ cup (12 T)	175 ml	6 fl oz
1 cup (16 T)	250 ml	8 fl oz
1¼ cups	300 ml	10 fl oz (½ pt)
1½ cups	350 ml	12 fl oz
2 cups (1 pint)	500 ml	16 fl oz
2½ cups	625 ml	20 fl oz (1 pint)
1 quart	1 liter	32 fl oz

Oven Temperature Equivalents

OVEN MARK	F	C	GAS
Very cool	250–275	130–140	½–1
Cool	300	150	2
Warm	325	170	3
Moderate	350	180	4
Moderately hot	375	190	5
	400	200	6
Hot	425	220	7
	450	230	8
Very hot	475	250	9

Acknowledgments

First books come with many debts. Whether they can be repaid or not remains to be seen, but at least here's a ledger to acknowledge the balance due.

I doubt I can ever repay Rozanne Gold for allowing me in to her home to work on a project that never materialized, sticking with me all these years, and pointing me in the right direction. Rozanne is one of the most generous people I have ever known. I'm proud to be one of the countless individuals she has helped to have a career in food.

No one could do better than having a publisher like STC. Leslie Stoker, thank you for having faith in a first-time author and hooking me up with the brightest and the best: Jennifer Lang, a superb editor, who got up to speed quickly and somehow managed to cheerfully pull me along; Laura Lindgren, an amazing designer who so "got it" I felt as though she was there when I wrote the book; Mark Thomas for his stellar photographs; copyeditor Pamela Mitchell, who had the very difficult job of taking scalpel to tender flesh (it wasn't so painful after all); Jack Lamplough; the entire sales and marketing department, and everyone who helps get books into the hands of the reader. You are all the best of the best.

Rachel Simon—let's see—you've been a teacher, colleague, mentor, and friend. Lynn Nusom is another stalwart mentor and friend. Thanks to both of you for giving me confidence. Maiken Scott belongs in this column, too, for bringing me aboard *Chef's Table* and teaching me about radio. Thanks, too, to our host Chef Jim Coleman. Michael Whiteman, thank you for being well read. I'd like to acknowledge my agent Gareth Esersky of the Carol Mann Agency for her efforts and for the term "recipe rescuer."

I owe all my neighbors for taking my turn at sidewalk clean-up, as well as giving my family attention when I wasn't. Thanks to Keith DiGiovanni for shoveling my walk during a blizzard when I was on deadline. Thanks to Kirsten McGregor and the Bannons for taking my many panic calls when I was short a testing ingredient and responding to the request to "throw a cup of flour over the back wall." Our block rocks!

Thanks to all the staff at WHYY who tasted all the recipes in various stages of deliciousness and noted some good suggestions. And thanks to the many recipe rescuers who opened their lives and their kitchens to me. Appreciation to Lisa Scottoline whose books have shown me what acknowledgments should be.

Most of all to Bill, who for years has supported me in every sense of the word. Without you I would never dared to dream, much less do it.

Index